TALKABOUT Sex and Relations

TALKABOUT Sex and Relationships 1 is a comprehensive toolkit for all therapists, educators and support staff who deliver relationship education to people with special needs. It is intended primarily to support groupwork but activities can be easily adapted to suit the needs of individuals with varying abilities. The resource emphasises the importance of happy, healthy and positive relationships. It looks at the life cycle of a relationship from finding a partner, coping with problems, staying safe and maintaining a relationship to dealing with the potential ending of a relationship.

This toolkit is the first in a two volume set, the second of which will focus on sex. Created by Alex Kelly and Emily Dennis as part of the bestselling TALKABOUT series, this publication constitutes the most complete and trustworthy set of resources available for groupwork focussing on relationships for people with special needs.

Alex Kelly is a Speech and Language Therapist and has supported people who have difficulties with their social skills, self-esteem and their relationships for thirty years. She is best known as the author of the hugely popular TALKABOUT resources which are practical books to help staff to develop children's social skills.

Emily Dennis has worked in learning disability since 2008 in a variety of settings: residential, supported living, day services and special education. In 2015 Emily joined Alex Kelly Ltd where she works as a project lead in sex and relationships.

TALKABOUT
Sex and Relationships 1

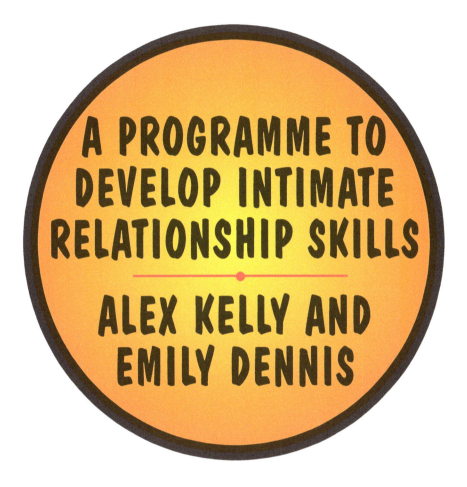

A PROGRAMME TO DEVELOP INTIMATE RELATIONSHIP SKILLS

ALEX KELLY AND EMILY DENNIS

Routledge
Taylor & Francis Group

LONDON AND NEW YORK

First published 2017
by Routledge
2 Park Square, Milton Park, Abingdon, Oxon OX14 4RN

and by Routledge
711 Third Avenue, New York, NY 10017

Routledge is an imprint of the Taylor & Francis Group, an informa business

British Library Cataloguing-in-Publication Data
A catalogue record for this book is available from the British Library

Library of Congress Cataloging-in-Publication Data
Names: Kelly, Alex, 1963– author. | Dennis, Emily, author.
Title: Talkabout sex & relationships 1 : a programme to develop intimate
    relationship skills / Alex Kelly and Emily Dennis.
Other titles: Talkabout sex and relationships one
Description: New York, NY : Routledge, 2017. | Includes bibliographical
    references and index.
Identifiers: LCCN 2016059005 | ISBN 9781138042506 (hardback) |
    ISBN 9781911186205 (pbk.) | ISBN 9781315173665 (ebook)
Subjects: LCSH: Interpersonal relations. | Social group work.
Classification: LCC HM1106 .K448 2017 | DDC 158.2—dc23
LC record available at https://lccn.loc.gov/2016059005

ISBN: 978-1-911-18620-5 (pbk)
ISBN: 978-1-315-17366-5 (ebk)

Typeset in Flora
by Apex CoVantage, LLC

Visit the eResources: www.routledge.com/9781911186205

Printed and Bound by Ashford Colour Press Ltd.

MIX
Paper from
responsible sources
FSC
www.fsc.org   FSC® C011748

Contents | Page

Acknowledgements viii

About the authors viii

Introduction to TALKABOUT Sex and Relationships:
a word from Alex Kelly 1

The theory behind the book: a word from Emily Dennis 1

An overview of the book 3

Assessment 13

Topic 1 Getting to know us

Activity 1 How am I feeling? 24
Activity 2 What is a relationships group? 26
Activity 3 This is a private group 30
Activity 4 Group rules 33
Activity 5 Who am I? 36
Activity 6 Linked together 40
Activity 7 This is me 41
Activity 8 Puzzle pieces 43
Activity 9 Who's who? 44
Activity 10 Fact finders 45
Activity 11 One nice thing 47
Activity 12 What's great about being us? 49

Topic 2 Staying safe

Activity 13 What does staying safe mean? 54
Activity 14 Safe/OK/dangerous 57
Activity 15 Safety snap 59
Activity 16 How do we stay safe every day? 64
Activity 17 Staying safe in relationships 68
Activity 18 What is abuse? 70
Activity 19 OK/not OK 73
Activity 20 OK/not OK pictures 79
Activity 21 OK/not OK . . . take two 84
Activity 22 What could I do? 87
Activity 23 What is consent? 92

Activity 24	What is trust?	99
Activity 25	Talk tech	101
Activity 26	Keep it real	104
Activity 27	Mystery mates	110
Activity 28	R U internet savvy?	115
Activity 29	Top tips for staying safe	117

Topic 3   Introduction to relationships

Activity 30	Which is which?	121
Activity 31	People in my life	127
Activity 32	Overlapping relationships	130
Activity 33	Qualities of a friend	132
Activity 34	Qualities of a partner	137
Activity 35	What is love?	140
Activity 36	Different types of love	142
Activity 37	What does love feel like?	144
Activity 38	Romantic rhymes	146
Activity 39	Roll with it	149
Activity 40	Mates or dates?	156
Activity 41	Relationship rules	159

Topic 4   Starting a relationship

Activity 42	What is attraction?	163
Activity 43	Love grows	166
Activity 44	Perfect pair	171
Activity 45	Larry looks for love	177
Activity 46	What should Larry say?	180
Activity 47	Cupid's clues	183
Activity 48	Fancy FACs	188
Activity 49	First date phases	190
Activity 50	Top tips for starting a relationship	192

Topic 5   Developing a relationship

Activity 51	Let it grow	196
Activity 52	Trust obstacles	197
Activity 53	The trusty detective	198
Activity 54	Supportive signs	204

Activity 55   Valuing a partner   211
Activity 56   Top tips for developing a relationship   214

Topic 6   Coping with problems

Activity 57   Problem partners   218
Activity 58   Conflicting couples   222
Activity 59   Conflict – what should I do?   224
Activity 60   Under pressure   227
Activity 61   Peer pressure – what should I do?   231
Activity 62   Jealous Jamal   232
Activity 63   Jealousy – what should I do?   235
Activity 64   Little white lies   236
Activity 65   Lying – what should I do?   240
Activity 66   Top tips for coping with problems   241

Topic 7   When a relationship ends

Activity 67   Why might a relationship end?   245
Activity 68   Emotional endings   250
Activity 69   Coping strategies   252
Activity 70   Heartbroken Henry   257
Activity 71   See-saw of love   259
Activity 72   Loving life   265
Activity 73   Top tips for a relationship ending   267

Topic 8   Looking to the future

Activity 74   In full bloom   271
Activity 75   Wonderful wishes   272
Activity 76   I have a dream   275
Activity 77   Compromising couples   277
Activity 78   Just around the river bend   279
Activity 79   Top tips for looking to the future   281
Activity 80   Certificates   283

Forms   285

References and further reading   289

Index   291

 **TALKABOUT**

 ## Acknowledgements

We would like to thank the following people for supporting us to write this book:

Amy Green – yet again we have to thank you for your support in bringing this book together. We couldn't have done it without you.

Rachel Harrison and Dave Raper from the University of Winchester – thank you for your time and advice and all those coffees in the VIP staff area!

Claire Lightley from the FPA – thank you for allowing Emily to attend your amazing training sessions and for your valuable feedback.

We would also like to thank everyone at Speaking Space. You continue to be an inspiration to us and we feel privileged to be part of your journey to independence. Thank you also for being part of the pilot for this resource and for your valuable feedback.

Finally we would like to mention our work colleagues who are all so lovely and supportive: Hannah Anderson, Joley Anderson, Grace Anstey, Amy Bigwood, Lisa Davidson, Marnie Daws, Abby Goodrich, Nevin Gouda, Amy Green, Rachel Hopkins, Amy Keable, Chris McLoughlin, Abbie Michael, Alec Morley, Zara Owens, Naomi Pearson, Helen Smith, Marina Trivett, Katherine Wareham and Rebecca Williams. We believe we are truly making a difference in everything we do and we want to thank you all for your enthusiasm, dedication and hard work.

This book is dedicated to everyone at Speaking Space.

About the authors

Alex Kelly is a Speech and Language Therapist with 30 years' experience of working with both children and adults with an intellectual disability (learning disability), and specialising in working with people who have difficulties with social skills. She runs her own business (Alex Kelly Ltd) with her husband Brian Sains and is the author of a number of books and resources, including the best-selling TALKABOUT series.

Alex Kelly Ltd is based in Hampshire, in the south of England. They provide training and consultancy work to schools and organisations in social skills, self-esteem and relationship skills around the UK and abroad. They also provide speech and language therapy in a number of schools in and around Hampshire. Finally they run a day service for adults called Speaking Space which aims to support people with social and communication skills difficulties through group work.

Emily Dennis has worked in learning disability since 2008 in a variety of settings: residential, supported living, day services and special education. Within these she worked as a Communication Coordinator delivering training and implementing communication systems across Hampshire. This included projects around service user empowerment, enabling vulnerable adults to assertively make clear and informed choices about their lives. At university Emily studied Social Care and specialised in learning disability and relationships. This led her to see the need for good quality, accessible sex education and become passionate about creating a programme that would enable this. In 2015 Emily joined Alex Kelly Ltd where she works as a project lead in sex and relationships.

You can contact Alex or Emily through the website **www.alexkelly.biz**

Introduction to *TALKABOUT Sex and Relationships*: a word from Alex Kelly

The original TALKABOUT book was first published 20 years ago following a clinical study of social skills that I completed between 1991 and 1995. It was the first social skills package to give people a hierarchy to work through from self-awareness to assertiveness. Since then, my work in this field has developed and increased, and, with this, so have the TALKABOUT products. Each TALKABOUT book is now aimed at a specific client group and has become more activity based with suggestions for games and activities for each topic. They are also more of a complete intervention package for teachers and therapists to use, including a scheme of work to follow throughout an academic year.

The other crucial development came in 2004 when I changed the hierarchy to include self-esteem and friendship skills. So the newer TALKABOUT books not only address self-awareness and social skills, but also self-esteem and friendship skills. And of course, I have always wanted to extend this to include intimate relationships but never felt I had the skill set to do this.

I then met Emily, who came to me with a proposal to increase the services we provide in our day service to include education in sex and relationships, and an idea was born! So for the past two years we have been busy . . . writing about sex and relationships, piloting our intervention and activities, and presenting to anyone who will listen to us on this subject. The result is too much to publish in one book, so we have divided it into two volumes: volume 1 is on relationships and volume 2 will be on sex education.

So this is the result of our work. We hope you like it but more importantly, we hope you find it useful.

Alex Kelly

Please feel free to contact me for more information or help with your work. My website is **www.alexkelly.biz**

The theory behind the book: a word from Emily Dennis

For many people with intellectual disabilities (learning disabilities), accessing accurate and unbiased sex education can be incredibly challenging. It is important to acknowledge how difficult and awkward it must be to ask a support worker or carer for information and advice on sex as it is an extremely personal and sensitive issue which many find embarrassing to discuss (Yacoub and Hall, 2009). Some people with learning disabilities therefore turn to their peers to ask questions about sex. Studies such as that by Yacoub and Hall have noted that there is often a great variation in knowledge and understanding of sex in people with learning disabilities. This may lead to these peers giving inaccurate, incorrect or contradictory information which could have dangerous consequences.

So what does history tell us about sex and people with a learning disability and how do we feel now, in today's society?

'Ordinary people leading ordinary lives' – this is the vision of people with learning disabilities in the 21st century. However, how do we really feel about adults with learning disabilities enjoying 'ordinary' sex lives?

Craft and Craft (1983) state that 'all humans have sexual drives' (Maslow, 1962, Wolfensberger, 1972). This is regardless of whether or not a person happens to have a learning disability. Craft and Craft (1982) also suggest that 'those who are mentally handicapped (sic) experience many of the same feelings and drives as the rest of the population, but commonly have been left in ignorance as to how to cope with them in a socially acceptable manner'. It could be argued that, in many cases, this is still happening today.

In the 1980s Craft and Craft identified the 'Pandora's Box Complex', which suggests that there is a fear that people are unable to deal with the complexities of sex. In some cases sex was never mentioned in case it unleashed uncontrollable urges and sterilisation was often seen as a solution.

Thankfully attitudes in society have moved forward a great deal since then. However, it is still the case that although 'people with mild and moderate learning disabilities have the same rights, [. . .] they do not enjoy the same opportunities, to enter into sexual relationships as anyone else' (Brown and Benson, 1995).

Often social care workers are not aware of the legislation and company policies (if available) surrounding the sexual relationships of the people they support. Murray et al. (1999; cited in Grieve et al., 2009) reported '47% of NHS staff and 16% of private sector staff were unsure or did not know their organisation's policies regarding client sexuality'. This study also found that 'a number of staff were also worried that that they could be disciplined, or even face prosecution if they condoned intimate relationships between people with learning disabilities in their care' (Grieve et al., 2009). 'Protecting people from all risks may seem like the safest thing in the short term, but can leave people more exposed to danger and abuse in the future' (Fanstone and Andrews, 2005).

Another consideration is sexual abuse and exploitation. As Fanstone and Andrews (2005) state: 'Sexual abuse and exploitation of people with learning disabilities is widespread and easy to cover up, leaving serious damage to people who are already "vulnerable"'. Firth and Rapley (1990) suggest that this makes it especially important to educate people with learning disabilities on their right to say no and methods of protecting themselves from this form of abuse. 'People with learning disabilities can be sexually exploited . . . the blame for this [is] largely [due to] the lack of sex education given to young people with learning disabilities' (McCarthy, 1999, p. 58). It is therefore of paramount importance that people with learning disabilities have the necessary skills, information and understanding to engage in sexual relationships without putting themselves, or others, in danger.

This means that sex education is a key component in keeping people safe but it is important to recognise that a single form of sex education may not be useful, accessible and understandable to everyone. There is no point in delivering sex education information which people cannot comprehend and is beyond their level of understanding (Cross, 1998). And you cannot just educate people in the facts around sex without firstly equipping them in the skills necessary to enjoy an intimate relationship.

For all these reasons, I feel passionately about the importance of sex and relationship education for people with learning disabilities and that this should be high quality, person-centred information available and accessible to all. So *TALKABOUT Sex and Relationships* is the result of many years of work in this field and aims to support and equip group facilitators and parents to address this stigma and hopefully to gain confidence to provide proactive, rather than reactive, sex and relationship education. In this way, we can hopefully reduce the risk of abuse, and support people with learning disabilities to have happy, healthy relationships and lead truly 'ordinary' sex lives.

An overview of the book

TALKABOUT Sex and Relationships is the first of two books. This one covers 'Relationships' and the second book covers 'Sex Education'. This is a practical resource that has been designed to help therapists and teaching staff to teach relationship skills in a more structured way, giving ideas on the process of intervention with lots of activities and worksheets to use at every stage. It is aimed at working with people in groups but can be adapted for working on a one-to-one basis. The book is divided into eight topics:

Assessment

This includes two assessments: a 1:1 interview and a friendship skills rating assessment. This provides you with a baseline score from which you can measure progress.

Topic 1 Getting to know us

This level helps the group to get to know each other using activities that will focus on self-awareness, self-esteem and group gelling.

Topic 2 Staying safe

This level introduces the concept of safety and how this relates to relationships.

Topic 3 Introduction to relationships

This level develops an understanding of different types of relationships: family, friends, professional, intimate and online.

Topic 4 Starting a relationship

This level introduces the concept of attraction and develops an understanding of where and how to meet someone.

Topic 5 Developing relationships

This level explores how relationships develop and teaches skills that are necessary to ensure this, including trust, support and valuing others.

Topic 6 Coping with problems

This level improves awareness into problems that may occur in relationships and teaches coping strategies such as: how to cope with jealousy, lying, peer pressure and conflict.

Topic 7 When a relationship ends

This level improves understanding into why relationships end and teaches coping strategies to deal with this and to move forward in their lives.

Topic 8 Looking to the future

This level explores dreams and wishes for the future both individually and as a couple. This includes learning to compromise and steps to achieve our goals.

Forms

In this section we have included formats for letters to parents/carers and session plans.

Who is TALKABOUT Sex and Relationships aimed at?

This resource is primarily aimed at young people or adults with a learning disability either in secondary education or adult services. We have piloted this resource with children in special schools (aged 13–18) and with adults (aged 18–35). However, we would extend this to include ages from 11 upwards depending on the individual.

When considering whether someone is suitable for this programme, it may help to ask the following questions:

- Do they struggle to make or keep friends?
- Are they isolated within their group?
- Do they struggle to understand appropriate relationships? E.g. what 'girlfriend/partner' means.
- Are they expressing interest in sex or intimate relationships?
- Are they exhibiting sexual behaviours?
- Are they vulnerable to sexual abuse?

The person should also have the following skills:

- Good self-awareness
- An ability to express themselves adequately in a group setting
- An ability to work within a group setting
- Motivation to attend a group

It is also important to remember that developing relationship skills should be seen within the context of the TALKABOUT hierarchy of intervention. This states that the pre-requisite skills of self-esteem and social skills should be taught prior to teaching sex and relationships.

The hierarchical approach to developing sex and relationships

Choosing the right place to start has to be the most important part of intervention as it is the difference between potentially setting someone up to fail or succeed.

Results from the social skills work in the early nineties led to the development of a hierarchy which is the basis of the TALKABOUT resources. It was found that the success of intervention increased if nonverbal behaviours were taught prior to verbal behaviours, and assertiveness was taught last. For example, children working on their verbal or conversational skills progressed more if they already had good nonverbal skills, and children working on their assertiveness progressed significantly more if they had existing good nonverbal and verbal skills. In addition, it was found that a basic self and other awareness was important to teach as a pre-requisite to social skills training. A hierarchy was therefore proposed, piloted and found to be highly successful.

The hierarchy of social skills

Awareness of self and others

↓

Nonverbal behaviour or foundation skills i.e. body language and paralinguistic skills

↓

Verbal behaviour i.e. conversational skills

↓

Assertive behaviour

This is logical. Think about conversational skills; they are more complex than the nonverbal behaviours. For example, consider listening: a good listener uses appropriate eye contact and facial expression to show he is listening. Now consider turn taking: this needs good listening which in turns needs eye contact, etc. So choosing the wrong skill to start work on, i.e. a skill that is too complex, will potentially set a child up to fail.

A few years later, a link was noticed between children and adults with social skills difficulties and those with low self-esteem and friendship skills difficulties. These three areas are often very interlinked. Low self-esteem can result in poor social skills. Poor social skills can result in a lack of friends. A lack of friends can result in low self-esteem. So the hierarchy was updated to include all three aspects of work.

The hierarchy of social skills, self-esteem and friendship skills

Self-awareness and self-esteem

$\downarrow$

Social skills (nonverbal, verbal and assertiveness)

$\downarrow$

Friendship skills (friendship skills, intimate relationship skills, sex education)

Using this hierarchical approach, teachers or care workers are able to start work with the person at a level that is appropriate to their needs and progress up the levels to enable them to reach their full potential.

This does mean that if someone needs work on self-esteem or social skills, then you may need to refer to another TALKABOUT book before you work on sex and relationships. You may find it helpful to use the following questions to guide you with this:

AREA OF NEED	NEEDS WORK?	TALKABOUT RESOURCE

Self-awareness & self-esteem...

Does the person have significant difficulties with their self-awareness or self-esteem?

NO   YES   →

Consider the need to start with

Talkabout for Children 1: Developing self-awareness and self-esteem (ages 11-16) or

Talkabout for Adults (ages 16+)

Social Skills...

Does the person have significant difficulties with body language or conversational skills?

NO   YES   →

Consider doing full assessment of social skills and if necessary start with

Talkabout for Children 2: Developing social skills or

Talkabout 2e

Friendship Skills...

Does the person have significant difficulties with friendship skills and would benefit from time spent developing this?

NO   YES   →

Consider starting with

Talkabout for Children 3: Developing friendship skills

Sex & Relationship Skills...

Does the person need to develop skills in sex and relationships?

NO   YES   →

Use

Talkabout Sex & Relationships 1: A programme to develop intimate relationship skills

Followed by

Talkabout Sex & Relationships 2: A programme to develop sex education

7

Setting up and running your relationships group

Here are a few guidelines for setting up and running your relationships group.

Group membership

It is important to match the group members in terms of their needs and also how well they are going to get on. A group is far more likely to gel and work well if they have similar needs, are a similar age and like each other. It is also important to consider gender of the group members and either have a single sex group or a group with a similar numbers of male/female members. Group membership should also be closed, i.e. you should not allow new members to join halfway through as this will alter the group dynamics.

The size of the group

Groups work best if they are not too small or too big, preferably between four and eight. I usually aim for a group of six. You need the group to be small enough to make sure that everyone contributes and feels part of the group and large enough to make activities such as role plays and group discussions feasible and interesting. Even numbers are helpful if you are going to ask them to sometimes work in pairs.

Length of the group

Timings are given at the beginning of each topic but it is important to remember that change will not happen quickly and you should allow time for group members to feel comfortable enough to talk about these issues. If you want to cover the entire content of this book, then you are probably looking at running the group for at least a year. In terms of the sessions, it is important that you have enough time to get through your session plan (see next section) but not so much time that the group members get bored. I usually aim for 45 minutes to 1 hour.

Group leaders

Groups run better with two leaders, especially as there is often a need to model behaviours, observe the group members, and facilitate group discussions. If you are able to have two group facilitators then ideally there would be one male and one female. This is not essential but can help with group discussions.

Accommodation

You will need a room that is comfortable for the group members to be in where you are not going to be interrupted. Don't be tempted to accept the corner of the hall or library as an acceptable place to run your group – this will not help your group members to relax and talk openly. In terms of the layout of chairs, I sometimes work around a table depending on the activity; however, it is usually helpful to start with the chairs in a circle for the group cohesion activity. I would also suggest that the group facilitators sit amongst the group members. I always place a 'private' sign on the door to let people know that a session is in place (see Activity 3) which can help the group members feel confident to speak out.

Cohesiveness

A group that does not gel will not learn or have fun. It is therefore important to take time to ensure that group gelling occurs. Things that help are:

- Interpersonal attraction – people who like each other are more likely to gel
- People who have similar needs
- Activities that encourage everyone to take part and have fun
- Arrange the chairs into a circle prior to the group
- Ensure that everyone feels valued in the group
- Ensure that everyone feels part of the group and has an equal 'say'
- Ask the group to set some rules
- Start each session with a simple activity that is fun and stress-free
- Finish each session with another activity that is fun and stress-free

The format of the session

The format of the session will vary from time to time but there are general guidelines which should be followed:

❶ Group cohesion activity

This is an essential part of the group. It brings the group together and helps them to focus on the other group members and the purpose of the group. The activity should be simple, stress-free and involve all.

❷ How are you feeling?

This should be done every session to ensure group members learn how to express their feelings and for the facilitator to address any concerns. Alternative feelings boards can be found in the *TALKABOUT for Children* 1 and *TALKABOUT for Adults* books.

❸ Main activity(s)

This will be your main focus of the session. It is during this part of the session that it is most important not to lose people's attention by allowing an activity to go on for too long, or one person to dominate the conversation.

❹ Finishing activity

Each session should end with a group activity to bring the group back together again and to reduce anxiety if the clients have found any of the activities difficult. The activity should therefore be fun, simple and stress free.

Abuse disclosure guidelines

Delivering work around sex and relationships may prompt disclosures of abuse. The group work provides a safe platform for this type of work and an environment to discuss negative experiences if they wish to.

As you work through the resource you will notice the warning symbol in the instructions of activities which may prompt a disclosure. The idea is this will enable facilitators to prepare themselves so if they were to receive a disclosure they can react calmly and confidently.

 Although facilitators should always be alert to the signs and signals of abuse, incidents may come to light during your sessions because a group member feels comfortable enough to disclose the information themselves. A disclosure can take place many years after the event or in an entirely different environment and it may be that the person now has the skills and confidence to share what has happened.

If someone discloses abuse to you:

Do

- Remain calm.
- Listen carefully.
- Be aware that medical evidence may be needed.
- Reassure the person that they did the right thing to tell you, and that you will inform the appropriate person and the service will take steps to support and protect them.
- Write down what the person has told you as soon as possible.

Do not

- Promise to keep secrets; you need to pass this information on to the appropriate person.
- Ask any leading questions.
- Press the person for more information.
- Stop someone who is freely recalling information. They may not tell you the information again.
- Discuss the disclosure with anyone other than those you have a legitimate need to know.

At the first opportunity write down, sign and date the disclosure.

You should

- Write down exactly what the person has told you, using their exact words and phrases if possible.

- Note the setting and anyone else who was there at the time.
- Describe the circumstances in which the abuse disclosure came out.
- Ensure you separate factual information from your own opinions.
- Follow your own organisational policies and procedures.

Measuring outcomes

It is always important to be able to measure the success of any programme and this is no exception. With any of the TALKABOUT programmes, we encourage group facilitators to use pre and post assessment data to show progress. For this programme, you can use the TALKABOUT Assessment for Relationships (pages 15–20) to show progress using the six-point rating scale:

1. **Skill not present** – They are not able to do this even with lots of prompting and support from you.

2. **Skill emerging with prompting** – They can do this but only after lots of support from you.

3. **Skill emerging with occasional prompting** – They can do this with a bit of support.

4. **Skill present in a structured situation** – They can only do this spontaneously in a structured setting.

5. **Skill present in some other situations** – They are able to do this in some other settings.

6. **Skill present and consistent across most situations** – They are be able to do this in any setting.

These scores can easily be transferred on to an Excel spreadsheet to show data for either an individual or for groups.

If you would like support in setting up, running or evaluating any of your work in this area, we can support you. We regularly run courses throughout the UK, and sometimes abroad, on assessing and teaching social skills, and developing self-esteem and relationships skills. We can also support you to become a centre of excellence in this area by helping you to measure and evidence the effectiveness of your work. Please contact us through our website: **www.alexkelly.biz**

(🧍) Assessment

Objectives	To provide a baseline assessment
Materials	1. 1:1 interview
	2. Relationship rating scale
Timing	The timing of the assessment will depend on how well you know the person. If you do not know them well, then you will need to talk to a number of people and gain their opinions on their strengths and needs.

Activity	Description
1. 1:1 interview	Use the questions below to help find out whether the person has difficulties with relationships. Make sure they feel relaxed and explain to them that you would like to ask them a few questions so that you can get to know them a bit better before you start working with them.
2. Relationship skill assessment	This is a rating assessment of a person's relationship skills. It is a six point rating scale from 1: skill not present to 6: skill present and consistent across most situations. There are three sections: staying safe, starting a relationship and relationship skills. Some of the information will come from your 1:1 interview with the person but some will require you to talk to people who know the person well and your own observations. These ratings can then be transferred on to the TALKABOUT Assessment Summary wheel to provide you with a visual representation of their strengths and needs.
Author note	It is important to remember that some of these skills require pre-requisite skills which include self-awareness and social skills. If you consider the person to have significant needs in these areas please refer to the TALKABOUT books for developing self-awareness (*TALKABOUT for Children 1* or *TALKABOUT for Adults*) and the TALKABOUT books for social skills (*TALKABOUT 2e*).

1:1 Interview

Name .... DoB ....

Completed by .... Date ....

---

1 Tell me a bit about yourself.

What do you like doing? What do you not like doing?

---

2 Tell me about your best friend.

Do you have someone who is your best friend? What are they like? Why do you like them?

---

3 Tell me about some other people who are important in your life.

E.g. girlfriend/boyfriend? Family?

---

4 Can you tell me what you look for in a friend?

Try to think of three qualities you would like your friend to have.

---

5 Do you find it easy to make friends?

Do you know what to say to them? Or questions to ask them?

---

6 If you wanted to make new friends, where could you go to make them?

---

7 How would you know that someone likes you or dislikes you?

What signs would you look out for?

(continued)

8 How could you show your friend that you really valued them?

What could you say or do to make them feel valued?

9 Sometimes things go wrong in a relationship. What could you do to make things better?

10 Sometimes relationships are not good for us and people can do things that are not OK. Can you think of anything that is not OK in a relationship?

11 Sometimes we feel unsafe. Can you think of situations or activities that could be unsafe if you weren't careful?

Think about around the home or out in the community.

12 If you felt unsafe, what would you do?

Is there someone you could talk to?

13 Sometimes the internet is not safe. Can you think of an example of what is unsafe?

Think about what you can share or not share.

14 Do you know what the word 'consent' means? Can you describe it to me?

15 Thank you for talking to me. Is there anything you would like to know about relationships?

STAYING SAFE	1 Skill not present *They are not able to do this even with lots of prompting and support from you*	2 Skill emerging with prompting *They can do this but only after lots of support from you*	3 Skill emerging with occasional prompting *They can do this with a bit of support*	4 Skill present in a structured situation *They can only do this spontaneously in a structured setting*	5 Skill present in some other situations *They are able to do this in some other settings*	6 Skill present & consistent across most situations *They are be able to do this in any setting*
1. **UNSAFE SITUATIONS** *Shows an awareness of unsafe situations e.g. crossing a road, using a hot oven*						
2. **STRATEGIES TO STAY SAFE** *Shows an ability to use appropriate strategies e.g. uses a level crossing, oven gloves*						
3. **TALKING TO PEOPLE** *Is able to identify appropriate people to talk to when they feel unsafe*						
4. **INTERNET BEHAVIOURS** *Is able to recognise unsafe behaviours when on the internet*						
5. **INFORMATION SHARING** *Is able to identify what is 'ok' and 'not ok' to share online*						
6. **CONSENT** *Shows an awareness of consent through appropriate behaviour e.g. will ask before kissing someone*						
7. **BEHAVIOUR AWARENESS** *Shows an awareness of 'not ok' behaviours within a friendship/relationship*						
8. **BODY AWARENESS** *Shows an awareness of their body and uses appropriate behaviour to stay safe*						

ASSESSMENT

STARTING A RELATIONSHIP	1 Skill not present _They are not able to do this even with lots of prompting and support from you_	2 Skill emerging with prompting _They can do this but only after lots of support from you_	3 skill emerging with occasional prompting _They can do this with a bit of support_	4 Skill present in a structured situation _They can only do this spontaneously in a structured setting_	5 Skill present in some other situations _They are able to do this in some other settings_	6 Skill present & consistent across most situations _They are able to do this in any setting_
1. **FORMING FRIENDSHIPS** _Is able to form new friendships appropriately and confidently_						
2. **DIFFERENT RELATIONSHIPS** _Understands the difference between friend, partner and other relationships_						
3. **IMPORTANT QUALITIES** _Is able to identify three qualities they would look for in a friend/partner_						
4. **MEETING NEW PEOPLE** _Can identify three appropriate places to go to meet new people_						
5. **CONVERSATION STARTERS** _Can appropriately initiate a conversation with different people_						
6. **ASKING QUESTIONS** _Can use questions appropriately to get to know someone_						
7. **RECOGNISING GOOD SIGNS** _Can identify three signs that someone likes them_						
8. **RECOGNISING BAD SIGNS** _Can identify three signs that someone does not like them_						

RELATIONSHIP SKILLS	1 Skill not present *They are not able to do this even with lots of prompting and support from you*	2 Skill emerging with prompting *They can do this but only after lots of support from you*	3 Skill emerging with occasional prompting *They can do this with a bit of support*	4 Skill present in a structured situation *They can do only this spontaneously in a structured setting*	5 Skill present in some other situations *They are able to do this in some other settings*	6 Skill present & consistent across most situations *They are able to do this in any setting*
1. **EXPRESSING FEELINGS** Able to tell others how they feel appropriately and assertively						
2. **VALUING OTHERS** Appears to value their friends/relationships through their behaviour						
3. **SHARING** Able to share appropriately within their friendships/relationships						
4. **PEER PRESSURE** Able to handle different types of peer pressure appropriately						
5. **TRUST** Demonstrates trustworthy behaviours in their current relationships						
6. **COMPROMISE** Shows an awareness of different opinions and how to compromise						
7. **JEALOUSY** Able to recognise and deal with the feeling of jealousy appropriately						
8. **CONFLICT** Able to use a variety of strategies to resolve conflict within a friendship/relationship						

© 2017, *Talkabout Sex and Relationships*, Alex Kelly and Emily Dennis, Routledge

 TALKABOUT sex and relationships summary

Name .... Date completed ....

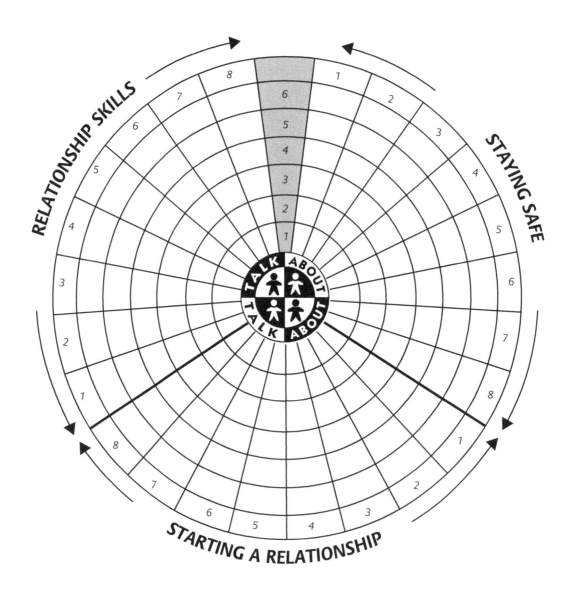

STAYING SAFE	STARTING A RELATIONSHIP	RELATIONSHIP SKILLS
1. Unsafe situations	1. Forming friendships	1. Expressing feelings
2. Strategies to stay safe	2. Different relationships	2. Valuing others
3. Talking to people	3. Important qualities	3. Sharing
4. Internet behaviours	4. Meeting new people	4. Peer pressure
5. Information sharing	5. Conversation starters	5. Trust
6. Consent	6. Asking questions	6. Compromise
7. Behaviour awareness	7. Recognising good signs	7. Jealousy
8. Body awareness	8. Recognising bad signs	8. Conflict

Topic 1 Getting to know us

Introduction

The aim of this topic is to help the group to get to know each other using activities that will focus on self-awareness, self-esteem and group gelling. Topics to be developed in future sessions will be introduced but the main objective of this topic is for group members to start talking about themselves and to feel comfortable with each other. This topic also introduces the activity 'How am I feeling?' and the 'private' sign which you will then use at the beginning of every session.

Objectives	• To introduce awareness of self and others.
	• To gel the group.
	• To get to know a bit about each other.
	• To introduce the activity 'How am I feeling?'
Materials	• Print out and laminate activities as appropriate.
	• You will need Velcro™ to make up some of the activities.
	• Print out and photocopy worksheets as appropriate.
Timing	• This topic will take up to 12 sessions to complete.

Activity	Description
How am I feeling? (Activity 1)	Pass the board around and ask each member to select how they are feeling. Can they share with the group why they are feeling that way?
What is a relationships group? (Activity 2)	The group complete mind maps on 'what are relationships?', 'what do I want to know?' and 'what would someone else want to know?' to introduce the topic. This will help to plan further group sessions.
This is a private group (Activity 3)	Using mind maps from Activity 2, the group discuss how these sessions should be private as you will be talking about sensitive issues. The group facilitator introduces the 'private' symbol and explains how it will be used in sessions.
Group rules (Activity 4)	Group members discuss and agree what they think the rules should be for this group to maintain confidentiality and for everyone to feel safe and comfortable.
Who am I? (Activity 5)	Cards are placed in the centre of the circle. Group members take it in turns to share something about themselves. Some of these ideas could be made into a group poster, for example 'These are the things that make us happy/sad/worried . . .'
Linked together (Activity 6)	A group gelling exercise where a ball of wool is passed round to people who have similar interests to see how group members are all linked together.
This is me (Activity 7)	The group can choose either to use a blank piece of paper or the head template to draw a self-portrait, adding qualities and facts about themselves. They then present this back to the group.
Puzzle pieces (Activity 8)	Photographs of group members' faces are enlarged to A4 and cut into puzzle pieces. The group then trades these to complete their face.

Activity	Description
Who's who? (Activity 9)	A personalised version of the game 'Guess Who' using photos of all the group members. Each person takes it in turns to try to guess who has been chosen from facts provided.
Fact finders (Activity 10)	Now the group has got to know each other, they complete a quiz with facts about each other.
One nice thing (Activity 11)	Stick a group member's photo in the centre of a piece of paper then go around the room with each person saying one thing they like about that person.
What's great about being us? (Activity 12)	The group complete the worksheet to look at how they are great as part of the group. What strengths do people bring to the group?

Activity 1 How am I feeling?

Preparation

Print out and laminate the feelings board. This board has five emotion choices and a question mark for 'other'. If you feel your group need a simpler or more complex board you could refer to *TALKABOUT for Adults*, *TALKABOUT for Teenagers* or *TALKABOUT for Children: Developing Self-Awareness and Self-Esteem* for more choices.

Instructions

- Introduce the emotions and the facial expressions.

- Pass the board around the group members and ask them to say how they are feeling. Encourage them to ask each other.

- Can they share with the group why they are feeling that way?

- The '?' is for people to choose another emotion that is not on the board, for example they may be feeling 'hungry' or 'lonely'.

- This works well as a starter activity for each relationships session.

Activity 1 How am I feeling?

Sad

Tired

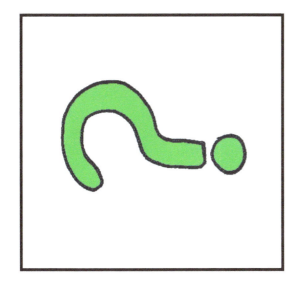

Worried

Happy

Angry

Activity 2 What is a relationships group?

Preparation

You can either enlarge the worksheets to A3 or use flipchart paper to write down ideas.

Instructions

- Explain to the group members that you are going to be starting a new group and that you would like ideas on how they feel about it.

- Ask the group: What are relationships? What different types or relationships can we think of? How are they different? Do they fit into different categories? Add answers to the sheet/ flipchart.

- What would they like to talk about? What questions do they have about relationships? What might someone else want to know? (A friend or a peer for example.) This can be used as a distancing technique if group members are embarrassed saying they would like to learn about it.

- Discuss relationships being a sensitive topic and that some people might feel a bit uncomfortable or embarrassed asking questions; this is ok. Relationships group is a safe space to ask questions.

Activity 2 What is a relationships group?

Name . . . .   Date . . . .

Getting to know us

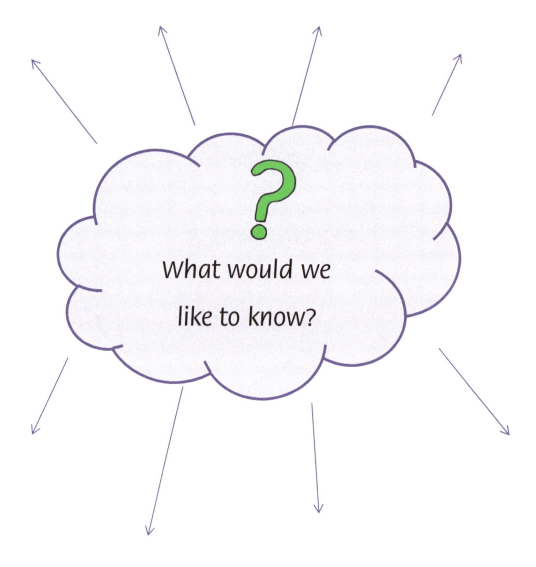

Activity 2 What is a relationships group?

Name . . . .   Date . . . .

What would we

like to know?

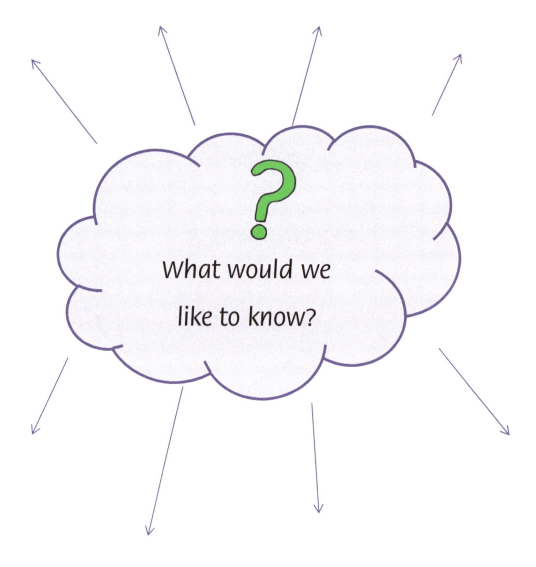

Activity 2 What is a relationships group?

Name . . . .   Date . . . .

What might someone else

want to know?

Activity 3 This is a private group

Preparation

Print and laminate the private sign so it can be attached to the door of the room where the group is held each session.

Print out a 'private' cover sheet for each group member with a photograph for their individual folders.

Instructions

- Remind the group of the previous activity and that some topics they discuss in the group may be of a sensitive nature. Reassure the group and remind them that what is talked about in relationships group should be private.

  NB – group facilitators should then say that they may have to discuss what happens in the group to other staff if needed.

- Show everyone the private sign and explain that a group member should attach this to the door at the start and end of each session.

- This acts as a cue to the session beginning and ending as well as a reminder to others to knock before entering the room.

- Group members should also cut and stick their photograph and write their name on the cover sheet for their folders. This will be a safe place to keep their work for the duration of the course.

Activity 3 This is a private group

Relationships Group

Relationships Group

Insert photo
here

Name:

This is my private folder

Activity 4 Group rules

Preparation

Print out the worksheets so each group member has a copy.

Instructions

- It is important to establish some rules so group members know what is expected of them in the sessions.

- The group should be encouraged to come up with the rules themselves, however, group facilitators should guide them towards covering the following:

    1. *Confidentiality* – What we talk about in relationships group should stay within the group.

       (However group facilitators may need to talk to other staff and pass on information if needed.)

    2. *Respect* – We should try to act and treat each other as adults.

    3. *Listening* – We should listen to one another and respect their ideas and opinions.

- Each group member should sign at the end to say they agree to try to keep to the group rules.

- The rules should be easily accessible in sessions; they could be on display on the wall, in group members' private folders or both. The group should also discuss what the consequence might be if someone breaks a rule.

Additional activity

If it would benefit the group you could complete a group contract. This can be especially useful if it is the first time the group has worked together.

You may also consider using a seating plan if you feel this will enable the group to be more productive.

Activity 4 Group rules

Name . . . .   Date . . . .

Relationship Group
Rules

○

○

○

○

○

○

We agree to try to keep to the rules we have decided on as a group. Signed...

Date:. . . . .

Activity 4 Group rules

Name . . . .   Date . . . .

Relationship Group Contract

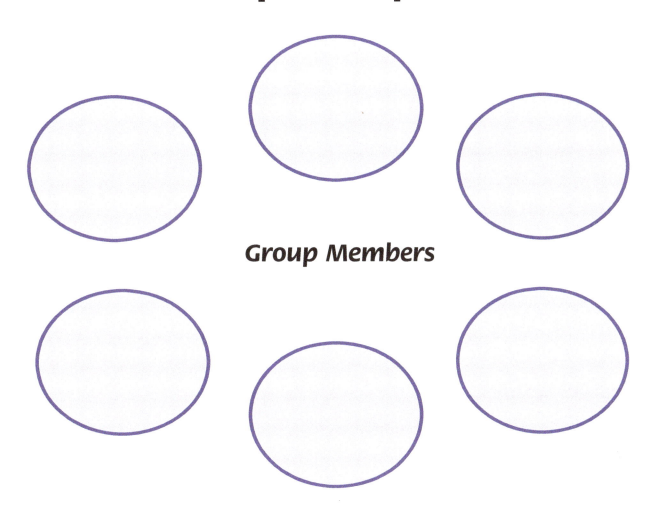

Group Members

We will meet every   . . . .

from . . . . to . . . .

at. . . . .

Activity 5 Who am I?

Preparation

Print and cut out the 'Who am I?' cards.

Laminate the cards if you wish to use them again.

Instructions

- Place the cards face down in a pile in the centre of the group.

- Group members take it in turns to select a card and share something about themselves by completing the sentence on the card.

- Continue until everyone has had a few turns.

- Next, ask the group to share their ideas on a few of the main cards for example by saying 'what makes us happy?' or 'what do we all like to eat?'

- Start with the easier topics such as things that make us happy or things we like to eat, then progress on to harder sentences such as things that make us angry or worried.

- The group then discusses what they have learnt about each other.

Additional activity

You may also wish to encourage group members to complete the 'Who am I?' worksheet afterwards to add to their folders.

Activity 5 Who am I?

I am happy when…	I get angry when…

I like to eat…	I hate eating…

My favourite day is…	I like to watch…

Activity 5 Who am I?

A nice thing about me is… 	My favourite place is… 
I worry about… 	My most treasured possession is… 
I am looking forward to… 	My favourite person is… 

Activity 5 Who am I?

Name: ....

Date: ....

I am ....
years old

My favourite colour is
....

I live in
....

Insert photo
here

My favourite music is
....

My hobbies are
....
....
....

My favourite food is
....

Activity 6 Linked together

Preparation

You will need a ball of wool or string.

Instructions

- Ask group members to stand in a circle facing inwards.

- The group facilitator will start by holding the ball of wool and giving a statement about themselves for example 'I love chocolate, does anyone else love chocolate?'

- The group facilitator then holds on to the end of the wool, but passes the ball of wool to a group member who agrees and also loves chocolate.

- It is now this person's turn to say a statement about something they like or dislike.

- They then hold on to their section of wool and pass the ball of wool onto the other person in the group who has the same likes/dislikes as they do. This continues for a while creating a web of connections and similarities between the group/circle.

- The facilitator should then prompt the group members to look around at the web the group has created to notice that we are all linked and have things in common.

Activity 7 This is me

Preparation

Group members can either complete a worksheet with the head template or use a plain piece of paper to draw a self-portrait.

You may also need a few mirrors so that group members can look at their reflection to help with drawing self-portraits.

Instructions

- Explain to the group that they are going to be thinking in more depth about themselves today, particularly what they look like.

- Each group member draws a self-portrait either on plain paper or using the head template.

- Encourage the group to spend time on their portrait, making sure they have included all details accurately such as their eye colour, hair colour and any glasses or jewellery, etc.

- The group then share their portraits and describe themselves.

Variation

As an additional activity you may want to enlarge the group members' portraits and support them to add labels describing themselves. This could include information about their age, personality, physical characteristics, things they like and things they love.

Alternatively, group members could draw and describe the person sitting opposite them.

Activity 7 This is me

Name: .... Date: ....

Activity 7 This is me

Activity 8 Puzzle pieces

Preparation

You will need photos of group members' faces, enlarged to A4, printed and laminated. They can be either cut into strips i.e. hair and eyes, nose, mouth or into a number of puzzle pieces depending on the ability of the group.

Instructions

- Each group member is given a hair and eye strip, a nose strip and a mouth strip. (If using the puzzle piece method, give each group member a pile of pieces.)

- Group members then trade strips (or puzzle pieces) with each other in order to complete their face. When trading, the group should be encouraged to take turns, ask questions and work out which strips (pieces) belong to whom.

Variation

Alternatively, the facilitator could put all the strips/puzzle pieces in a pile in the centre of the group. Group members take it in turns to call out 'pick up if. . .' statements, such as 'pick up if you have a brother', 'pick up if you have a pet dog', etc. Continue until each person has a completed puzzle.

Activity 9 Who's who?

Preparation

You will need an old 'Guess Who' board game or similar. You will also need additional photographs of group members and others, for example staff and other students to increase the choice. However remember to ask permission if you are going to do this.

You will need to print and laminate three copies of each person (one for each board and one loose in a bag) and resize them to slot into the game. This takes a while to make but is a great personalised game that can be used in a variety of groups!

Instructions

- One person chooses a card from the bag of loose pictures.

- Group members then take it in turns to ask questions and find out who the person has chosen.

- The group will need to use good self and other awareness skills to do this activity and should be encouraged to all ask an appropriate question.

Variation

You could take photos of people dressed in disguise or fancy dress for example, wearing wigs, scarves, jewellery, etc., and then show these to the group and work out who is who.

Activity 10 Fact finders

Preparation

Print out a fact finders worksheet for each person with a photograph of someone in the group (including facilitators).

Instructions

- Encourage group members to think back to other activities they have completed in this module, for example 'Who am I?', 'This is me' and 'Linked together'.

- Hand out the Fact Finders worksheets; make sure that nobody gets a sheet with their own photo on.

- Group members should then see what facts they can remember about the person they have on their sheet.

- Once group members have completed as much as they can remember, they can then ask the rest of the group if anyone else can remember any more facts.

- Once everyone has finished and has had help from the group they can then check the facts with the person on their sheet. How many correct answers does each person have?

Additional activity

Place photographs of group members face down in the centre of the group. Each group member should then take it in turns to pick up a photo but not show the rest of the group. They will then introduce this person such as on a TV show, for example 'Next up we have a very fashionable lady from Salisbury, she is amazing at ballet, terrified of spiders and loves eating fish and chips! It's . . . X!' The group all clap as this person stands up and takes a bow.

Continue until each group member has had a go.

Activity 10 Fact finders

Insert Photo Here

Name:

....

Age:

....

Lives in:

Favourite food:

Favourite colour:

Favourite animal:

Favourite music:

Hobbies:

Any pets?

Dislikes:

Things we have in common:

Activity 11 One nice thing

Preparation

You will need several sheets of flipchart paper and photographs of each group member.

Instructions

- Each piece of flipchart paper should have a photograph of a group member stuck in the centre. You should focus on one person at a time. Choose someone to begin with.

- Take it in turns to go around the room and say one thing each group member likes about that person.

- Continue until each person has a page full of compliments about themselves.

- Read out each person's page and give them a round of applause.

Variation

The group decides which person they will start with. Pass around a blank piece of paper. Group members take it in turns to write one nice thing, then fold the piece of paper so the next person cannot see what has already been written. Continue until you have done this for each person and then read them out to the group.

Additional activity

Group members should complete the worksheet individually, writing their qualities on to the thumb and fingers of the 'thumbs up' picture. If people find it difficult to think of things to write you could prompt them to think back to what group members have said in previous activities.

Activity 11 One nice thing

Name: ....   Date: ....

I am great because....

Activity 12 What's great about being us?

Preparation

Use a sheet of flipchart paper or enlarge the worksheet to A3. Work on the activity as a group then photocopy the page so each group member has a copy for their private folder.

You can choose whether or not you include group facilitators in this activity.

Instructions

- Take it in turns to think of why it's great to be part of this group.

- Do we feel differently to when we first started working as a group several weeks ago?

- What have we learnt about each other?

- Who has similar interests?

- Why are we a brilliant group?

- You may wish to decorate this page and create a poster to have on display where you run the group.

Our Group...

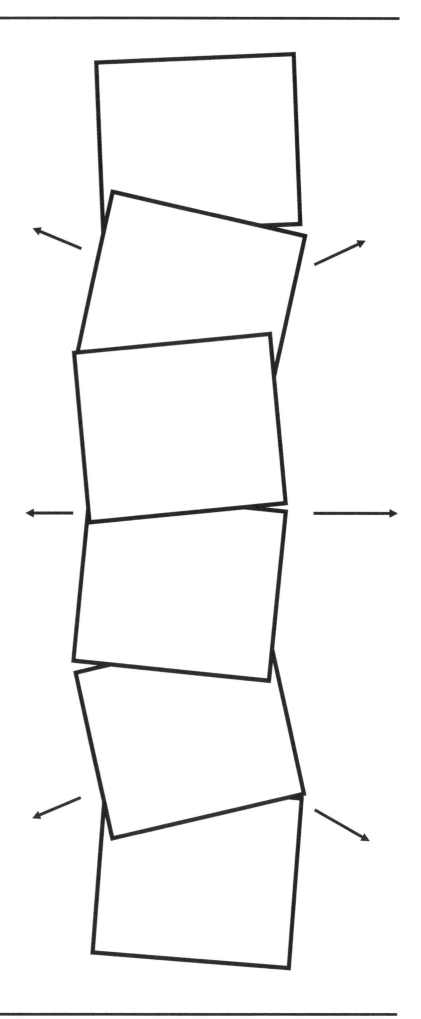

Topic 2 Staying safe

Introduction

The aim of this topic is to start discussing the concept of safety. What is safety in a wider context then how this relates to relationships? What is acceptable/ unacceptable (OK/not OK) in a relationship and what could we do about this? The chapter will look at recognising potentially dangerous situations and how to respond.

Objectives	• To introduce safety in the context of relationships.
	• To recognise safe and unsafe situations.
	• To know the early warning signs for feeling unsafe.
	• To know what to do if you feel unsafe.
	• To learn who and how you should tell people if you feel unsafe.
Materials	• Print out and laminate activities as appropriate.
	• You will need Velcro™ to make up some of the activities.
	• Print out and photocopy worksheets as appropriate.
Timing	• This topic will take up to 17 sessions to complete.

Staying safe

Activity	Description
What does staying safe mean? (Activity 13)	Introduce the concept of 'safe' to the group through a mind map exercise. The group then discuss what 'safe' feels like and create a collage.
Safe/OK/dangerous (Activity 14)	An activity where the group find images of safe and dangerous situations and rate them on a scale.
Safety snap (Activity 15)	A snap type activity where the group aim to match situations and safety equipment.
How do we stay safe every day? (Activity 16)	The group think about their morning routine and how they stay safe at each point. The group discuss similarities and differences.
Staying safe in relationships (Activity 17)	The group think about the different parts of a relationship and what they may need to think about to stay safe.
What is abuse? (Activity 18)	A mind map activity is used to get the group thinking about what abuse means and the six different types of abuse.
OK/not OK (Activity 19)	The group vote on different scenarios thinking about whether they are 'OK' or 'not OK'.
OK/not OK pictures (Activity 20)	The group consider eight different scenario pictures and whether they are 'OK' or 'not OK'. They will also discuss how people may feel in these situations.
Ok/not OK . . . take two (Activity 21)	Now the group are familiar with the OK/not OK voting system they will explore more explicit scenarios.
What could I do? (Activity 22)	The group sort good and bad ideas for dealing with a situation. A scenario is then broken down and group members decide on a solution using the good ideas.
What is consent? (Activity 23)	The group read through three stories introducing the concept of consent. They then decide on a definition.

Activity	Description
What is trust? (Activity 24)	The group discuss what trust means and decide on a definition. They then think about three people they trust in their lives.
Talk tech (Activity 25)	An activity which finds out which technology group members use and the pros and cons for each.
Keep it real (Activity 26)	Scenario cards are read as a group and sorted into 'Friend' or 'Online friend'. The group then discuss this issue with the use of an information worksheet.
Mystery mates (Activity 27)	The group facilitator reads a story about two women who meet online. The group discuss how safe the situation is and what should be done instead.
R U internet savvy? (Activity 28)	Following the previous session around internet safety, group members create a sheet of their tips for staying safe online.
Top tips for staying safe (Activity 29)	To end the topic, the group create their top tips for staying safe in a relationship.

Activity 13 What does staying safe mean?

Preparation

Either print A4 worksheets for each person or enlarge the worksheet to A3 to discuss as a group. You could also use a piece of flipchart paper to collect ideas.

You may wish to use images from the internet or magazines to describe 'safe'. Group members could be involved in collecting these.

Instructions

- Encourage the group to think about and discuss:

  1. What does 'safe' mean? What does it feel like?

  2. What things do we do to stay safe? (Think about safety equipment, signs and rules, etc.)

  3. How can we stay safe?

- Group members should then cut and stick any photos or images they associate with feeling safe on to their 'What does safe feel like?' worksheet.

- Depending on the group's ability they could also cut and stick words they might think of in relation to feeling safe. These may include words such as 'protected', 'secure', 'relaxed' and 'loved'.

- You may wish to use faces from the feelings board to cut and stick on to worksheets as well.

- Discuss how 'safe' feels slightly different for each of us.

Activity 13 What does staying safe mean?

Name: ....   Date: ....

What does safe

mean?

 **Staying safe**

 Activity 13 What does staying safe mean?

Name: ....   Date: ....

'Safe' feels like...

Activity 14 Safe/OK/dangerous

Preparation

You may need to have the worksheets from previous activities out to help recap on what 'safety' means.

You will also need to collect a number of images of different situations and objects that could be classed as safe, ok or dangerous. For example a motorbike, cliff jumping, watching TV, etc.

Instructions

- Place the images you have found face down in the centre of the group.

- Group members should take it in turns to pick an image and discuss where they think it should go on the scale from 'safe' to 'dangerous'.

- Remember, this may be different for each person. For example, one person might associate a dog as a family pet and companion who makes them feel safe and comfortable, other people may have had a bad experience and are terrified of dogs so would rate them as dangerous.

- This could be discussed as a group and either voted on or compromised and put in the middle ('OK').

- Can anyone think of other 'safe' or 'dangerous' situations?

Activity 14 safe/OK/dangerous

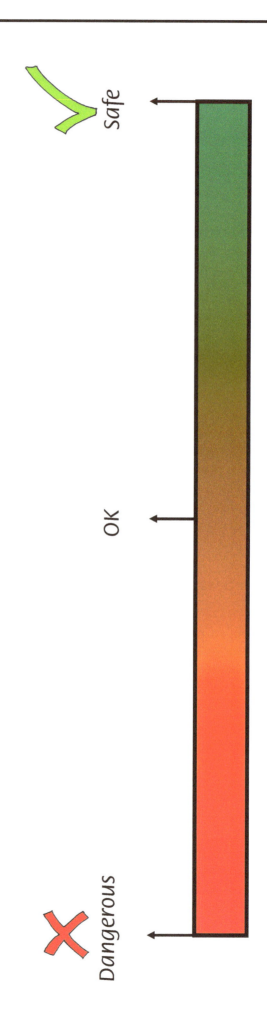

Safe

OK

Dangerous

Activity 15 Safety snap

Preparation

Print, laminate and cut out the safety snap cards.

Instructions

- This activity could be used as a group cohesion/starter activity for some groups; other groups may need to spend a bit more time discussing the concept of safety.

- Split the cards into the situations, e.g. swimming, bike, night time, and the safety equipment e.g. floats and goggles, helmet and torch. Place each pile face down in the centre of the group.

- Group members take it in turns to pick up two cards and see if they match, for example 'car' and 'seatbelt'. If they do they shout 'snap' and then get to keep those cards. If not the cards go the bottom of the piles and the next person has a turn.

- Continue until all cards have been matched.

Additional activity

The group could come up with ideas of new snap cards for different situations, for example sky diving and a parachute.

Activity 15 Safety snap

Car 	Seatbelt 
Bike 	Helmet 
Cooking 	Oven gloves 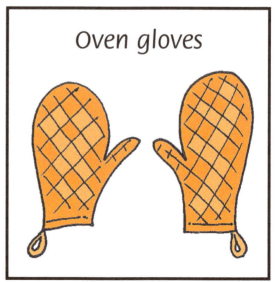

Activity 15 Safety snap

Science

Safety goggles

Sun

Sun screen

Night time

Torch

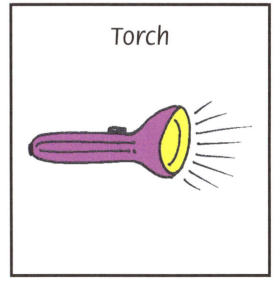

Activity 15 Safety snap

Boat	Life jacket

Football	Shin pads
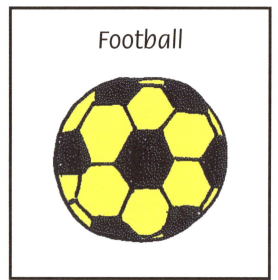	

Injury	Plaster
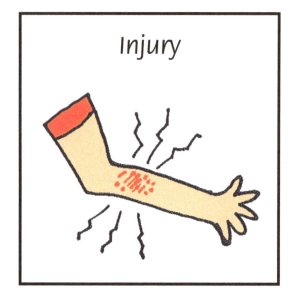	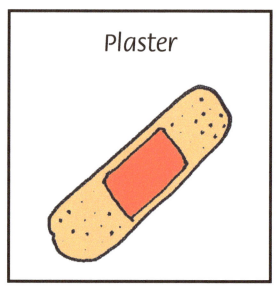

Activity 15 Safety snap

Swimming 	Goggles / floats 
Fire 	Fire alarm 
First date 	Mobile phone 

Activity 16 How do we stay safe every day?

Preparation

Print and cut out a set of the morning routine cards for each person. You will also need sheets of A3 paper.

Instructions

• Begin by asking the group to sort the cards into the right order of their morning routine.

• This may be different for each person and some cards will not be applicable. Discuss the differences in the group.

• Using a sheet of A3 paper, each group member should make a timeline of their daily routine, sticking on the pictures in the correct order.

• Once everyone has completed this, choose one person's timeline and discuss how we stay safe while doing each of these activities, making notes on the timeline. For example, do you need support in the shower, is there a non-slip mat?

• If this person's timeline has not used some cards that others have, discuss what you would need to stay safe for these too.

• If appropriate, sensitively discuss the differences in the group. Mention that we all have our own strengths and weaknesses. Something which is easy for one person may be difficult for another and vice versa.

Variation

Alternatively you could use a piece of string and peg up the morning routine cards in the right order.

Activity 16 How do we stay safe every day?

Sleeping

Wake up

Alarm clock

Brush hair

Shower

Bath

Activity 16 How do we stay safe every day?

Wash hair

Wash

Dry hair

Get dressed

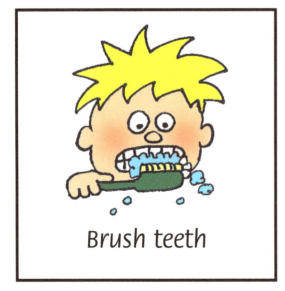

Brush teeth

Breakfast

Activity 16 How do we stay safe every day?

Cup of tea

Coffee

Pack your bag

Make your lunch

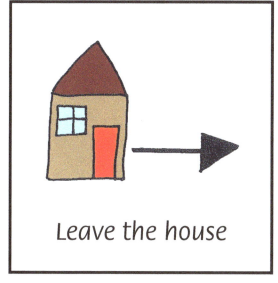

Leave the house

Get in your taxi

 ## Activity 17 Staying safe in relationships

Preparation

Print out the worksheets either in A4 for individual work or A3 if doing this as a group activity.

Instructions

- Introduce the session by reminding the group of the previous activity where they thought about staying safe in their morning routine. This time they are going to do the same thing but for a relationship.

- Group members begin completing the worksheet by thinking of different aspects/parts of a relationship and listing these in the left-hand column.

- They then add ideas of how we would stay safe for each part/aspect in the right-hand column. For example, on a first date you would tell a friend where you were going and what time you would be back.

- Group members should then feedback their ideas to the group and discuss.

Activity 17 Staying safe in relationships

Name: ....

Date: ....

Parts of a relationship	? What could I do to stay safe?

Activity 18 What is abuse?

Preparation

Print out the worksheets either in A4 for individual work or enlarge to A3 if doing this as a group activity. Alternatively you could write ideas on a piece of flipchart paper.

Instructions

• Explain to the group that they will be considering a new topic today, abuse.

• Begin by asking the group if anyone knows what 'abuse' means and adding ideas on to the mind map worksheet.

• Next, ask the group if they can give any examples of different types of abuse. Add these to the sheet also. You could prompt with the category cards or other ideas if necessary.

• The group should also decide on a definition of abuse to write in the box at the bottom. They can either think of their own or look it up in a dictionary or online.

Variation

The group could complete their worksheets individually and then share ideas at the end.

© 2017, *Talkabout Sex and Relationships*, Alex Kelly and Emily Dennis, Routledge

Activity 18 What is abuse?

Name: .... Date: ....

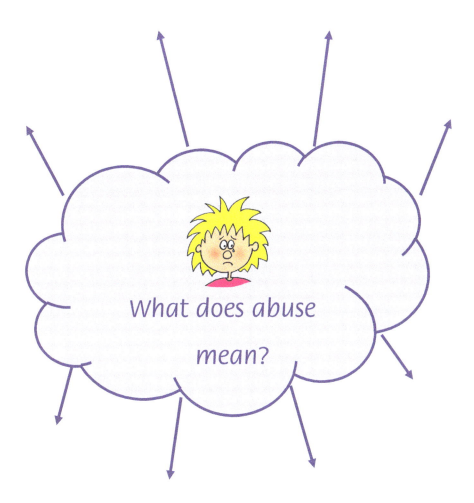

What does abuse mean?

Abuse is ....

....

....

Activity 18 What is abuse?

If someone wants to hurt you or cause you pain

If someone is rude or nasty to you

If someone touches a part of your body you do not want them to

If people do not look after you

If someone makes you feel scared or unsafe

If someone takes your money or things and does not return them

Activity 19 OK/not OK

Preparation

Print out and laminate the 'OK' and 'Not OK' cards enough for group members to have one of each. You could stick them to lollypop sticks so group members can hold them up to vote if they think a situation is 'OK' or 'Not OK'. Also print the 'OK', 'Not OK' heading cards and laminate if you wish to use them again.

Instructions

- The group facilitator introduces the cards and then explains that they are going to read some scenarios to the group and everyone must vote for each one if it is 'OK' or 'Not OK'.

- After each scenario group facilitators should encourage group members to discuss why they thought the scenario was 'OK' or 'Not OK'. How did it make them feel?

- Discuss any differences of opinion within the group.

- The scenarios can then be placed under the correct 'OK' or 'Not OK' heading.

Variation

Depending on the group's reading skills, you may wish to put all the scenario cards in the centre; group members then take it in turns to choose a card, read it out, and get the group to vote.

Alternatively, the group could look at some short clips from TV soaps. Discuss what is happening. What are the different characters doing? How do you think they are feeling? Is this 'OK' or 'Not OK'? What could the characters do differently to make this OK?

Activity 19 OK/not OK

OK	Not OK
OK	Not OK
OK	Not OK

Activity 19 OK/not OK

Activity 19 OK/not OK

Paula hugs Barry. They are friends	Amanda shakes hands with her new care manager.
Sally's support worker Tom gives her a kiss on the lips.	Jenna hits Paul. It really hurt Paul.
Jasmine shouts at Fran and slaps her face.	Seb trips over and bumps into Mary. It was an accident but Mary is upset.
Claudia shoves Sue. Sue falls over.	Neil and Peter are playing a wrestling game and are pretending to fight. Peter hits Neil on the arm. Neil laughs.

Activity 19 OK/not OK

Dan's carer keeps calling him silly names. Dan feels upset.	Sophia called Brenda a fat cow. Brenda is crying.
Simone carries Keith's wallet in her hand bag to go to the shops. Keith does not have any pockets.	Ben keeps taking Phil's money. Phil doesn't know.
Amy has forgotten her purse. Emily lends her some money to buy a sandwich.	Jon rings Rita for a chat. Rita hasn't got time to talk at the moment, she has to rush to get to her Doctor's appointment.
Every time Mike goes out with his support worker they go to the cinema and Mike has to pay. Mike hates the cinema.	Terry needs help in the shower. His dad says he is too busy to help him.

Activity 19 OK/not OK

Lizzie's mum gives her cold baked beans for dinner. She has had baked beans for dinner every night this week.	Hannah has gone to her day service without her packed lunch. This is the third time this week.
Frankie's mum never buys her clothes. All her clothes are now old and ripped.	Harry's mum is working late today. They don't have dinner until 8 o'clock.
Leah's mum has forgotten to wash her dress. Leah is going to a party and wants to wear it.	Liam and Toby are playing football. Liam tackles Toby and hurts his leg. Liam says sorry.
Vicky hits Bella with a folder.	Rosa is dancing and accidently hits Jimmy when she swings around. Jimmy is upset.

Activity 20 OK/not OK pictures

Preparation

You will need the 'OK' and 'Not OK' voting cards and headings from the previous activity.

Print and cut out the 'OK/Not OK' pictures. You may wish to laminate these if you will be using them again. You may also like to enlarge them so that everyone in the group can see clearly.

Instructions

- The facilitator should introduce the pictures one at a time and place them in the centre of the group.

- Group members should discuss what they think is happening. What are the different characters doing? How do you think they are feeling?

- They can then vote, is this 'OK' or 'Not OK'? Group members discuss any differences in opinion before placing them under the appropriate 'OK' or 'Not OK' header.

Staying safe

Activity 20 OK/not OK pictures

Activity 20 OK/not OK pictures

Activity 20 OK/not OK pictures

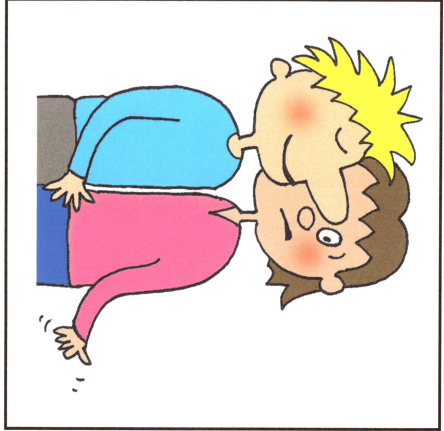

Activity 20 OK/not OK pictures

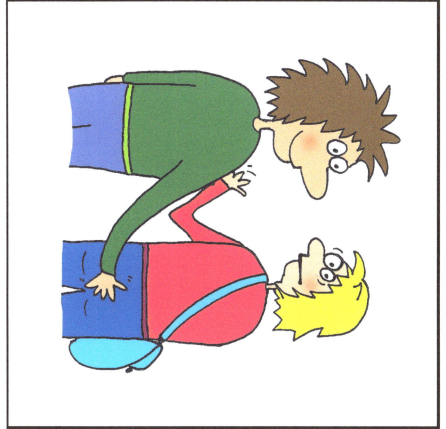

Activity 21 OK/not OK . . . take two

Preparation

Print and cut out the more explicit situation cards. You may wish to laminate these if you are using them more than once.

You will need the 'OK' and 'Not OK' voting cards and headings from Activity 19.

Instructions

- Read out the following scenarios to the group and ask them if they feel they are 'OK' or 'Not OK'.

- Ask group members to vote with their 'OK' or 'Not OK' cards.

- After each scenario, group members discuss why they feel the scenario was 'OK' or 'Not OK'.

- The scenarios can then be placed under the correct heading.

Please note

It is important for the group to do a fun finishing activity before the session ends in case anyone has felt anxious after completing this activity.

Activity 21 OK/not OK . . . take two

Robin touches Donna's bottom. Donna does not like it.

Ronnie touches Judy's bottom. Judy likes it.

Tyrone touches Wayne's bottom.
Wayne likes it.

Georgie's support worker keeps asking her to touch his private parts. She does not want to.

Jordan wants to have sex with Rachel. Rachel wants to have sex with Jordan. They are excited.

Jessica keeps showing Natalie her private parts. Natalie does not like it.

Joshua wants to have sex with Mel. Mel does not want to have sex. Joshua offers to give Mel money to have sex.

Gordon wants to have sex with Bert. Bert wants to have sex with Gordon. They are excited.

Activity 21 OK/not OK . . . take two

Graham and his support worker are having sex.	Sanjay asks Cathy if he can touch her private parts. Cathy says yes. Cathy is happy. Sanjay is happy.
Pippin's support worker has been taking photos of her when she is naked.	Martin's support worker shows him videos of people having sex on his computer.
Nancy and Norman kiss and cuddle. Nancy is happy. Norman is happy.	Tim and Henry kiss and cuddle. Tim is happy. Henry is happy.
Violet is sad because her dog has just died. Her support worker gives her a hug.	Deryck asks Daisy if he can touch her private parts. Daisy says not today because she feels unwell. Deryck says sorry. They watch TV instead.

Activity 22 What could I do?

Preparation

Print, cut out and laminate the 'Good idea' and 'Bad idea' headings and the idea cards.

You will need a scenario to discuss. You could use one from Activities 19 or 21. Alternatively, you could find a TV clip, soaps work well.

Print out the comic strip worksheets. They should be A4 for individual use or enlarged to A3 for group work.

Instructions

- Place the heading cards in the centre of the table and ideas cards face down in a pile.

- Group members take it in turns to pick an idea card and decide if it is a good or bad idea, placing it under the right heading.

- Continue until all of the cards have been sorted.

- The facilitator should then read out/show the scenario.

- Following the structure of the comic strip worksheet, break the scenario down into different stages/parts of what happened.

- Group members should start by thinking about 'who', 'where' and 'when' the situation started then fill in what happened.

- The group should also consider how are the characters feeling and add this to the heart in each box. What did they say? What did they do? What went wrong?

- Group members should now discuss how the characters could have done things differently using their 'good ideas' as prompts.

- The group should then re-write the comic strip with these suggestions using the second worksheet to create a solution.

Activity 22 What could I do?

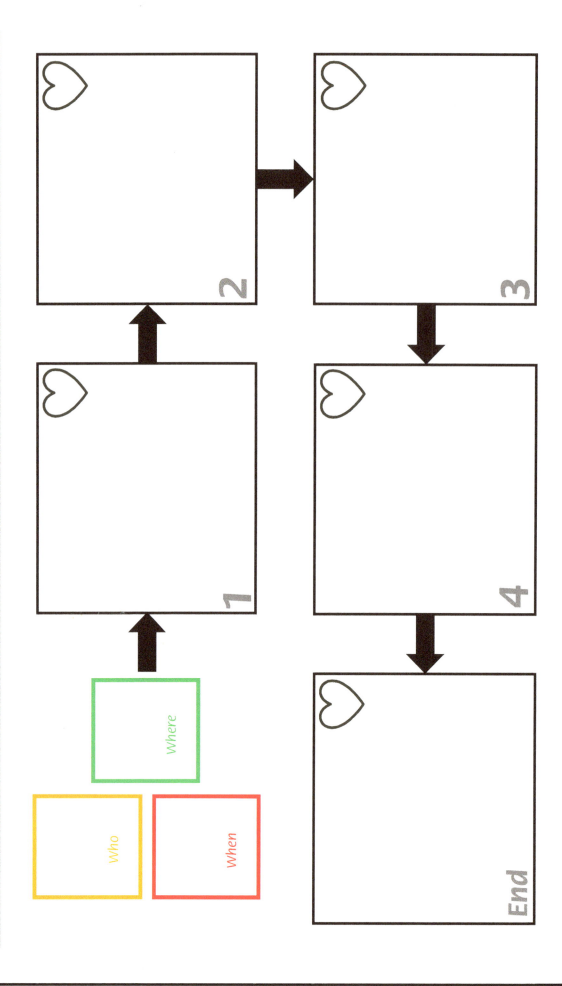

Who

Where

When

2

3

1

4

End

Activity 22 What could I do?

Solution...

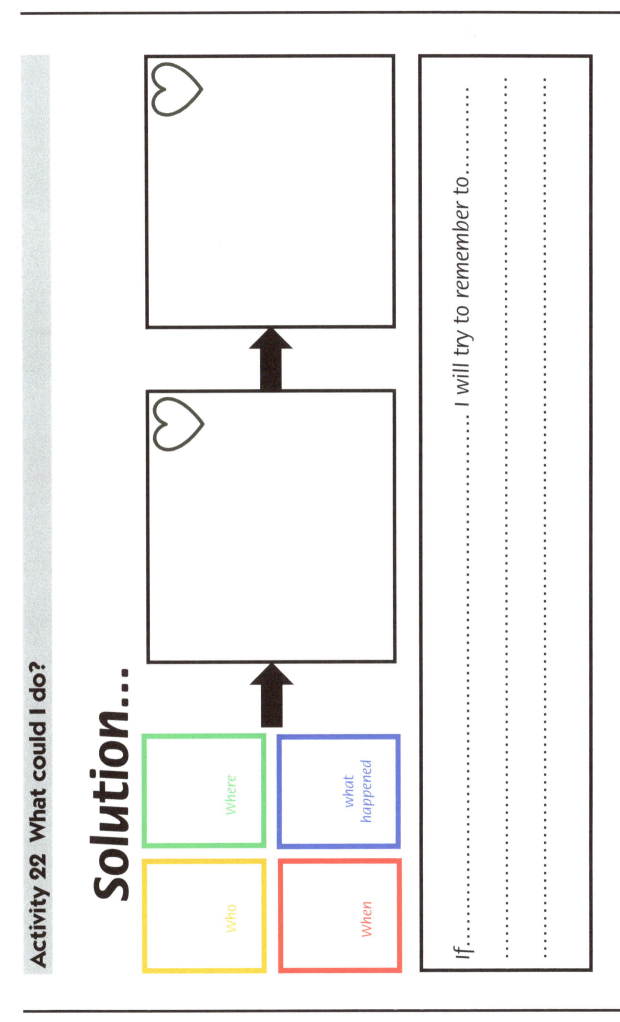

Who

Where

When

what happened

If ....

... I will try to remember to ....

Activity 22 What could I do?

Good ideas

Bad ideas

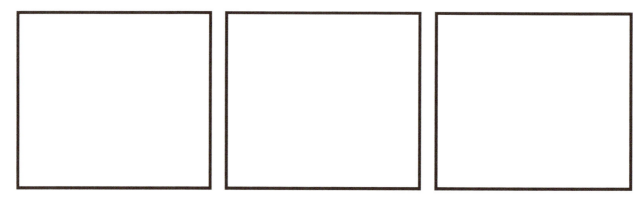

Activity 22 What could I do?

Hide	Talk to someone	Say NO
		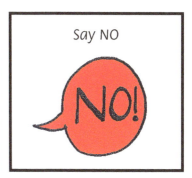

Shout	Don't do anything	Take time out
	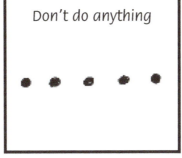	

Think	Hit someone or something	Ask for help

Count to 10	Run away	Say how you feel

Ask for a hug	Keep it a secret	Call the police

Activity 23 What is consent?

Preparation

The stories of consent, names and action cards should be enlarged to A3 and laminated. Attach Velcro™ to each of the boxes on the stories and opposing Velcro™ on to the name (blue) and action (green) cards.

You may also choose to use the 'OK' and 'Not OK' voting cards from Activity 19.

Instructions

- The group facilitator will explain to the group that they will be looking at the topic of consent today and reading a few stories.

- The group facilitator should start with 'The story of consent . . . take one' and attach the names and 'To have a cup of tea' actions into all the relevant boxes. Begin with a heterosexual couple and make sure the last action is the 'Have a cup of tea' label so that the story makes sense.

  NB – name/person cards are edged in blue and should be attached to the blue boxes on the stories. Action cards are edged in green and should be attached to the green boxes.

- Ask the group how they feel about the story; is it OK or not OK?

- Change the characters so they are now a homosexual couple. Ask group members to vote again, does this change anything?

- Now change the action, perhaps the couple are now kissing or holding hands. The group should vote and discuss again.

- The facilitator should then create and read out 'The story of consent . . . take two' asking the group to listen carefully to see what has changed. You may wish to start with the simplest couple and action as above and then swap the characters and actions discussing the differences. Again, ask the group to vote; do they feel the situation is OK or not OK and why.

- Continue with 'The story of consent . . . take three'. Discuss with the group how you would feel if someone ignored you and made you do something you did not want to do.

- Three themes should emerge from the activity, story one will always be OK (regardless of the characters and actions) because the couple are consenting. Story two will always be OK because one character has said they don't want to do something, the other person has listened and respected their decision, and so not done the action. Story three is never OK; we should never make someone else do something they don't want to. This can be as

simple as having a cup of tea but it is especially important when we think of more intimate actions within a relationship.

- Following on from the stories group members should complete the consent worksheet.

- Discuss if and where group members have heard of it before and in which situations. Does it have the same meaning as it does when talking about relationships?

- As a group, decide on a definition for consent and add this to the box at the bottom of the worksheet. The group can either think of a definition themselves or look one up online or in a dictionary.

Adapted from a video by Thames Valley Police, 2015

Activity 23 What is consent?

This activity consists of cards to be cut out, arranged in five rows. Each row contains name cards and action cards:

Row 1 (blue name cards): Jennifer · Johnny · Toby · Kathryn
Row 1 (green action cards): Touch · Kiss · Hug · Have sex · To hold hands · To have a cup of tea · Have a cup of tea

Row 2 (blue name cards): Jennifer · Johnny · Toby · Kathryn
Row 2 (green action cards): To touch · To kiss · To hug · To have sex · To hold hands · To have a cup of tea

Row 3 (blue name cards): Jennifer · Johnny · Toby · Kathryn
Row 3 (green action cards): To touch · To kiss · To hug · To have sex · To hold hands · To have a cup of tea

Row 4 (blue name cards): Jennifer · Johnny · Toby · Kathryn
Row 4 (green action cards): To touch · To kiss · To hug · To have sex · To hold hands · To have a cup of tea

Row 5 (blue name cards): Jennifer · Johnny · Toby · Kathryn
Row 5 (green action cards): To touch · To kiss · To hug · To have sex · To hold hands · Hold hands · To have a cup of tea

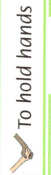

Activity 23 What is consent?

A story about consent… Take one!

_____ wants _____

with _____

_____ asks _____ "would you

like?" _____

_____ wants _____

with _____ .

_____ says "yes, I would like

_____ ".

_____ and _____

_____ .

 **Activity 23 What is consent?**

A story about consent... Take two!

	wants	

with | |

| | asks | | "would you

like | |

| | does not want

| | with | |

| | says "no, I do not want

| ".

| | and | | do not

| .

Activity 23 What is consent?

A story about consent...Take three!

[_____] wants [_____]

with [_____]

[_____] asks [_____] "would you

like [_____]

[_____] does not want

[_____] with [_____]

[_____] says "no, I do not want

[_____]".

[_____] ignores [_____] and

makes them [_____].

Activity 23 What is consent?

1. **Ask** the other person

2. **Listen** to them

3. **Respect** their decision

Remember

It is ALWAYS ok for someone to change their mind!

Activity 24 What is trust?

Preparation

Print out a copy of the worksheet for each group member.

Group members should also be encouraged to bring in three photographs of people they trust.

You may need a piece of flipchart paper and pens for writing ideas.

Instructions

- The group facilitator should introduce the session explaining that the group are going to start a new topic today, trust.

- The group should think about and discuss what they think trust is. Ideas should be added to the large piece of paper. Consider the following:

  1. What does trust mean?

  2. Who do we trust in our lives?

  3. How do we know if someone is trustworthy?

- Group members then complete their individual worksheets by sticking the photographs of three people they trust and adding their names.

- As a group, decide on a definition for trust and add this to the box at the bottom of the worksheet. The group can either think of a definition themselves or look one up online or in a dictionary.

Activity 24 What is trust?

Name: ....   Date: ....

Insert photo here	Insert photo here	Insert photo here
....	....	....

If I had a worry or felt unsafe, I could talk to…

Trust means…

Activity 25 Talk tech

Preparation

Print, laminate and cut out the internet safety cards. You will also need to print the survey sheet.

Instructions

- Place the internet safety cards face down in the centre of the group.

- Take it in turns to pick a card and call out either 'hands up if. . .', 'stand up if. . .' or 'change places if. . .'. Choose whichever the group would be most comfortable with.

- Continue until all cards have been used.

- Next complete the group survey.

- Write the names of group members at the top of the sheet. Take it in turns to ask another member of the group which technology they use. You can also extend your table to include any other devices or apps group members use regularly.

- Once everyone's information has been recorded, feedback to the group which is the most popular and least popular technology.

- The group should then discuss what each piece of technology is for, what is good about it, what is not so good or could be potentially dangerous.

Activity 25 Talk tech

…if you use a laptop	…if you use a computer

…if you use a tablet	…if you use a smart phone

…if you use social media	…if you play online games

Activity 25 Talk tech

 Tick to show who uses what

Names: ➡						
Laptop						
Computer						
Tablet						
Smart Phone						
Social Media						
Online Games						

Activity 26 Keep it real

Preparation

Print off the 'Real friend'/'Online friend' heading cards and situation cards. You may wish to laminate these if you will use them more than once.

Print off a prompt sheet for each group member.

Instructions

- Place the 'Real friend' and 'Online friend' heading cards in the centre of the group and place the situation cards face down in a pile.

- Group members should take it in turns to pick a card and decide whether the characters are real friends or online friends. The group member should then place the card under the appropriate heading. Discuss any differences in opinion.

- Once this activity is completed the facilitator should then hand out the 'Real friend vs online friend' fact sheet and discuss it.

- Next, refer back to the previous activity and look on the group survey to see how many people use social media.

- Ask the group to look at how many friends they have on social media. How many of these are our friends in real life? Use the worksheet to look at one of the friends as an example and test it out.

Additional activity

Using the photo frame worksheet, group members should try to think of two friends, one they know in real life and one who they are friends with online. Can they draw them? Which friend is easier to draw? Why?

Alternatively there are a number of awareness raising videos online which you could show to the group and discuss.

Activity 26 Keep it real

Activity 26 Keep it real

Cecil

You were in the same class as Cecil at School. Your mums are friends and you see him most weekends.

Mike

You talk to Mike most evenings on an online game. He's the same age and likes the same things as you.

Dominique

Dominique has recently started coming to your Day Service. She is very friendly and you get on well.

Debbie

Debbie is a big fan of your favourite band. You love talking about them on social media.

Paul

Paul used to be your next door neighbour. He moved to Australia last year but you regularly email and Skype each other.

Laura

Laura has all the best posts on social media. She's cool, fashionable and leads a glamourous lifestyle.

Activity 26 Keep it real

Danny Danny goes to swimming club with you every Thursday. You have a good laugh together.	**Rodney** Rodney added you on Facebook a few weeks ago. He's really friendly and wants to meet up at the weekend.
Georgia Georgia works the library with you on Saturdays. You enjoy chatting to her in the staff room at lunch time.	**Mary** You met Mary on an online game. Your characters are friends on the game and you've recently started instant messaging.
Freddie Freddie likes all your posts on social media. He always says lovely things, like how pretty you are in photos.	**Angela** Angela works at the local shop. You always chat to her when you pay for your shopping. She is polite and friendly.

Activity 26 Keep it real

Name: ....   Date: ....

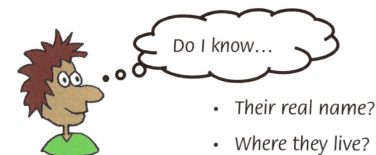

Do I know...

- Their real name?
- Where they live?
- Their family?
- When their birthday is?
- What they look like?

Watch Out!

You must never tell an online friend any personal details like where you live, bank details, phone numbers and passwords.

Do we...

- Work together?
- Go to the cinema together?
- Go to the same Day Service?
- Chat face to face?

Remember!

Sometimes people use fake names, ages and photos online. They could be somebody completely different!

Don't forget!

You should never do anything online that you would not do in real life!

Activity 26 Keep it real

Name: ....

Date: ....

 ## Activity 27 Mystery mates

Preparation

Print and laminate a stop sign for all group members. You may wish to attach these to sticks so they can easily be held up.

Print the story and laminate if you wish to use it again.

Instructions

- Explain to group members that you will read through a story. The group facilitator should pause when there is a question in bold, ask the group and discuss answers. Then continue with the story.

- If group members start to feel that Ellie is not being safe in the story, they should hold up their stop sign.

- Group members should try to explain why they feel the situation has become unsafe and why they used their 'stop' sign.

- Continue to the end of the story and discuss what has happened as a group.

© 2017, *Talkabout Sex and Relationships*, Alex Kelly and Emily Dennis, Routledge

Activity 27 Mystery mates

Ellie and Pippa

Ellie loves playing online games. It's great fun and she has made lots of new friends. Pippa is one of her best friends online. She makes Ellie laugh. They are both 25 and like the same music.

Ellie logs onto her social media page. She has a friend request from Pippa.

Should she accept the friend request?

Ellie looks at Pippa's social media page. There are a few photos of a girl in her 20s. She seems nice. Ellie writes on Pippa's wall "Thanks for the add! ☺"Later on Pippa "likes" some of Ellie's photos.

Later that day Ellie goes onto social media again. She has a private message from Pippa.

> Hi Ellie!
>
> Love your photos! Your pet cat is so cute!
>
> Pippa x

> Hello!
>
> Thanks! Sometimes she's cute but she's only a kitten so she's quite naughty at times! Ellie x

> Haha! I bet! I have a kitten too! Her name is Bella, she's a tabby. Where do you live? Would you like to come and see her sometime? Pippa x

Activity 27 Mystery mates

Should Ellie tell Pippa where she lives?

> Oooh!! I'd love to!! I live in Brighton. Where do you live? Ellie x

> No way!! I live in Brighton too! Would you like to come over at the weekend? My kitten hasn't had all her jabs yet so can't leave the house. What's your phone number? Pippa x

Should Ellie share her phone number?

Should Ellie go to Pippa's house?

> That would be great! What's your address?
> My phone number is 01234 56789.
> Text me the details! Ellie x

Should Ellie have given her phone number to Pippa?

A text comes through from Pippa.

> I live at 41, Sea View, Brighton. You should come over after work! Don't worry about telling your mum. She knows we are friends, it will be fine.
> Pippa x

Should Ellie check with someone she trusts?

Should she go to Pippa's house?

Activity 27 Mystery mates

> Ok, great! I'll be over at 5.30.   Ellie X

> Can't wait!   ☺   Pippa x

Do you think Ellie should be doing this?

Ellie finishes work. She texts Pippa to let her know she's on her way.

> Just leaving, see you in 10 minutes!   Ellie x

> Yay! Can't wait to finally meet you!   Pippa x

Ellie arrives at Pippa's house. Should she ring the doorbell?

Ellie rings the doorbell

The door opens. Standing in the doorway is a man.

> "Oh hi, you must be Ellie! Would you like to come in and see my cat?"

What's wrong? What do you think has happened?

How is Ellie feeling? Should she go in and see the cat?

> Sorry, I must have the wrong house. I'm looking for my friend Pippa.

> No, this is the right house. I'm your friend Pippa.

What do you think has gone wrong? What should Ellie do?

What can we learn from this story?

Activity 27 Mystery mates

Activity 28 R U internet savvy?

Preparation

Print out an individual A4 worksheet for each group member.

Instructions

- Discuss what you have learnt as a group over the last few activities around staying safe online.

- The group then consider what their top tips for staying safe online would be. They can either write their own tips and then share with the group or work in pairs.

- Tips that people could include are: never share personal details, think carefully before posting photos, report things online that are offensive or upsetting, talk to someone if you see something that worries you.

- The group could then share their tips with each other. These posters could then be displayed near computer access points to raise awareness if appropriate.

Activity 28 R U internet savvy?

Name: .... Date: ....

My tips for staying safe online...

-
-
-
-
-
-

Activity 29 Top tips for staying safe

Preparation

Worksheets should be printed A4 for individual work or enlarged to A3 for a whole group activity.

Instructions

- The group should come up with a list of top tips for staying safe, thinking about the skills practised in the whole topic:

  - Staying safe

  - Staying safe in relationships

  - Abuse

  - OK/not OK situations

  - Consent

  - Trust

  - Online safety

- You may wish to discuss these as a group first or group members can complete the sheet individually then share ideas after.

- They can then place them in their private work folder.

 **Staying safe**

Activity 29 Top tips on staying safe

Name: .... Date: ....

Top Tips

- ○
- ○
- ○
- ○
- ○
- ○

Remember:

Topic 3 Introduction to relationships

Introduction

This topic looks at different types of relationships that we have in our own lives as well as those in wider society. Groups will discuss friends and their qualities; what makes a great friend? They will then relate this to good qualities in a partner and what we should look for.

Objectives

- To introduce different types of relationship.
- To recognise which of these relationships we have and how they are different.
- To recognise good qualities in a friend.
- To think about the qualities we would like a potential partner to have.
- To think of relationship rules to enable us to have safe relationships.

Materials

- Print out and laminate activities as appropriate.
- You will need Velcro™ to make up some of the activities.
- Print out and photocopy worksheets as appropriate.

Timing

- This topic will take up to 12 sessions to complete.

Introduction to relationships

Activity	Description
Which is which? (Activity 30)	The group is introduced to a new topic, looking at different types of relationships. They read through a number of scenarios and sort them into different categories.
People in my life (Activity 31)	The group complete a worksheet looking at the different types of relationships they have in their own lives.
Overlapping relationships (Activity 32)	A Venn diagram activity is used to look at how relationships may fit into more than just one category. Scenarios from Activity 30 are revisited to help explain this.
Qualities of a friend (Activity 33)	The group rates the qualities of a friend they feel are most and least important using a thermometer worksheet. They then choose their top qualities of a friend.
Qualities of a partner (Activity 34)	Similar to the previous activity, the group rate which qualities they think are most important in a partner using the thermometer and then complete a lonely hearts worksheet with their top choices.
What is love? (Activity 35)	This exercise introduces the concept of love. The group make a poster of words and images they associate with love and find a definition.
Different types of love (Activity 36)	The group consider different characters' relationships in their favourite television programme and sort them into the correct 'love category'.
What does love feel like? (Activity 37)	The group look at what love feels like in terms of emotions, thoughts, body reactions and actions and complete a worksheet with ideas.
Romantic rhymes (Activity 38)	Group members read different idioms and metaphors we associate with love and then try to match these to the real meaning.
Roll with it (Activity 39)	An activity where group members roll two dice, one with people and one with actions, then vote to indicate whether they feel this is an 'OK' or 'Not OK' interaction.
Mates or dates? (Activity 40)	A sorting activity where the group decide what activities friends might do together and what activities a couple might do. Is there a difference?
Relationship rules (Activity 41)	Group members write a list of rules for their folders around the key to a good relationship.

Activity 30 Which is which?

Preparation

Print, cut out and laminate the heading cards and scenarios.

Instructions

- Introduce the new topic and explain to the group that they will be looking at different types of relationships today.

- Place the heading cards in the centre of the group explaining each one as you go. Place the scenario cards face down in a pile.

- Take it in turns to pick a card and read the scenario aloud to the group.

- The group member then chooses which category the scenario should go under and explains why.

- Discuss as a group, do we agree or disagree? Why?

- Continue until all scenarios have been sorted.

Additional activity

You could use a variety of TV clips showing different relationships. This could be done in the session or, depending on the group's ability, it could be a homework task. You could give each person a category, for example professional. The group member then finds a clip and shows it to the group the following session.

Activity 30 Which is which?

Activity 30 Which is which?

Sharon and Dr White

Sharon sees her doctor once a month to monitor her medication. Dr White is always very nice to her.

Senita and Jack

Senita lives on her own, but needs help with her shopping once a week and with managing her money. Jack is paid to help her for five hours a week. They get on well.

Poppy and Simon

Poppy and Simon like to meet up and go for a drink at their local pub. They have similar interests and always have good fun. Poppy has a boyfriend, and Simon is gay.

Sue and Harmeet

Sue is a nurse. She visits Harmeet at home as he has been ill and checks his medication every day. Harmeet likes Sue.

Judy and Mary

Judy and Mary are sisters. They have always got on well, and spend lots of time together, often shopping. Judy has just started working for Mary.

Toby and Liam

Toby is Liam's boss. They work closely together, but do not like each other.

Activity 30 Which is which?

Tom and Kristina

Tom met Kristina through a mutual friend, and they have been having sex for nine months. They are thinking about living together.

Mavi and Bill

Mavi and Bill met at football, but no longer play for the same club. They are both gay, and have had sex a couple of times, but neither wants a permanent relationship.

Alf and Skyla

Alf and Skyla are in the same class at school. Alf really fancies Skyla and wants to ask her out. They seem to get on well and neither of them has a partner at the moment.

Patricia and Brody

Patricia and Brody met each other through online dating. They have been talking for three months but have not met up.

Sherman and Claire

Sherman and Claire met on social media through a mutual friend, Jasper. They talk every day and have got to know each other really well.

Shanice and Roger

Shanice and Roger met in a book club. They get on well and fancy each other, but have not done anything about it. Shanice is married, and Roger is single.

Introduction to relationships

Activity 30 Which is which?

Chezene and Andy

Chezene attends a local college, and Andy is one of her tutors. Chezene has a crush on Andy.

Justin and Katrina

Justin and Katrina play in a band together. They have known one another since they were at school.

Cheng and Lin

Cheng and Lin are brother and sister. Cheng is 21, and is four years older than his sister Lin. Cheng is very protective of Lin.

Sheila and Neil

Neil and Sheila are married. They have two children.

Fergus and Harry

Fergus is Harry's uncle. Harry does not like Fergus, and has not seen him for several years.

Jude and Sam

Jude and Sam live in a house with two other adults. They have sex with one another, but have not told anybody about their relationship.

Introduction to relationships

Activity 30 Which is which?

✂

Gabby and Satwinder Gabby met Satwinder through a mutual friend. They go out drinking and clubbing, as part of a larger group of friends.	**Keenan and Arnold** Keenan and Arnold are cousins. They live in different countries and have never met but talk online regularly.
Luc and Jasmine Luc and Jasmine both play online games and have recently added each other as "friends".	**Joseph and Fiona** Joseph and Fiona are engaged. They do not want to have sex until they are married.
Donald and Monique Donald is English, and Monique is French. Donald is living with Monique's family for a few weeks, as part of a school exchange.	**Tyrone and Tamsin** Tyrone is Tamsin's nephew. Tyrone lives in America, and Auntie Tamsin lives in England. They video call each other regularly, and see one another every two years.

© 2017, *Talkabout Sex and Relationships*, Alex Kelly and Emily Dennis, Routledge

Activity 31 People in my life

Preparation

Each group member will need a worksheet enlarged to A3 and a set of cards. You may need to print additional blank cards.

Group members should be encouraged to bring in photographs of their friends and family for this activity.

Instructions

- Explain to the group that today they are going to be looking at the different types of relationships they have in their own lives.

- Group members are each given a set of cards and are asked to stick photographs or draw pictures of their family and friends on to the blank ones. They will also write the names below.

- They then decide how important that person is to them and stick the card on to their worksheet as appropriate. They will then look at the additional cards such as 'Dentist', and add these on too.

- Continue until all cards have been added.

- The group then share their sheets and discuss similarities and differences as a group.

Activity 31 People in my life

Activity 31 People in my life

Name: ....   Date: ....

Important to me...

Activity 32 Overlapping relationships

Preparation

You will need a worksheet enlarged to A3.

Alternatively you may wish to use three hoops overlapping on the floor if you are doing this as a group activity.

You will also need the scenario cards from Activity 30.

Instructions

- Explain to the group that sometimes relationships don't fit neatly into just one category. Often we find that some overlap.

- Place the worksheet or hoops in the centre of the group.

- Place the scenario cards from Activity 30 face down in a pile.

- Group members take it in turns to pick a card and read it aloud to the group. They then consider where they would place it on the worksheet.

- The rest of the group then discuss if they agree with this, why or why not.

Additional activity

The group could also look at the people they used in Activity 31 and discuss if any of these relationships overlap in their own lives.

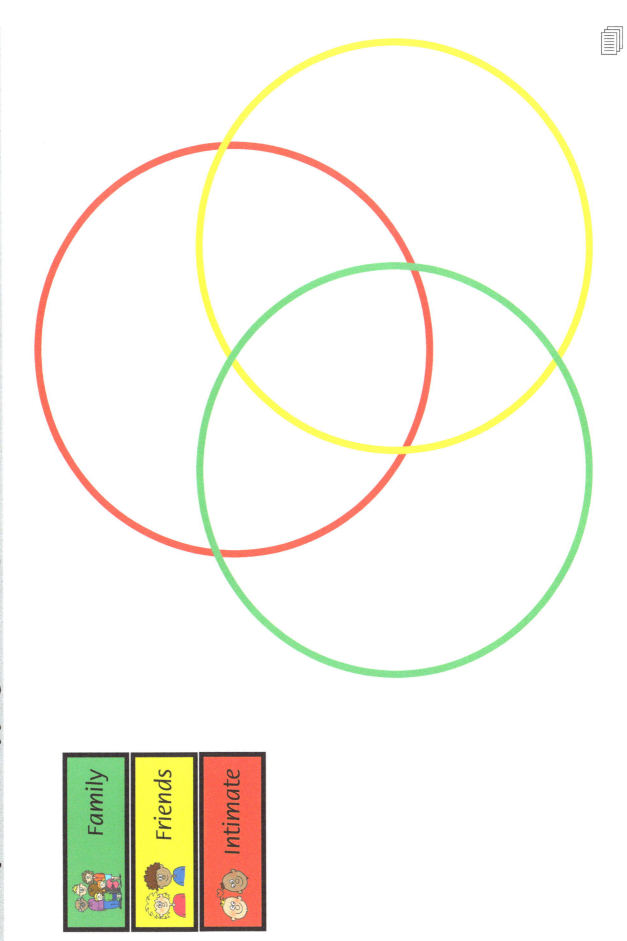

Activity 32 Overlapping relationships

Family

Friends

Intimate

Activity 33 Qualities of a friend

Preparation

Print, cut out and laminate the qualities and put them into a bag or hat.

Print the thermometer worksheet and enlarge to A3.

Print out a copy of the lonely hearts worksheet and a copy of the qualities on A4 for each group member.

Instructions

- The facilitator should explain the thermometer scale and that the rating goes from very important to not important at all.

- Group members take it in turns to pick a quality from the bag/hat and place it on the thermometer depending on how important they feel it is.

- They should then discuss why they have chosen to place it there.

- There will be different opinions in the group, reassure the group that this is ok and discuss them.

- Group members then complete a lonely hearts worksheet, cutting and sticking their top four qualities they look for in a friend into the spaces provided. They could then share these with the rest of the group.

Activity 33 Qualities of a friend

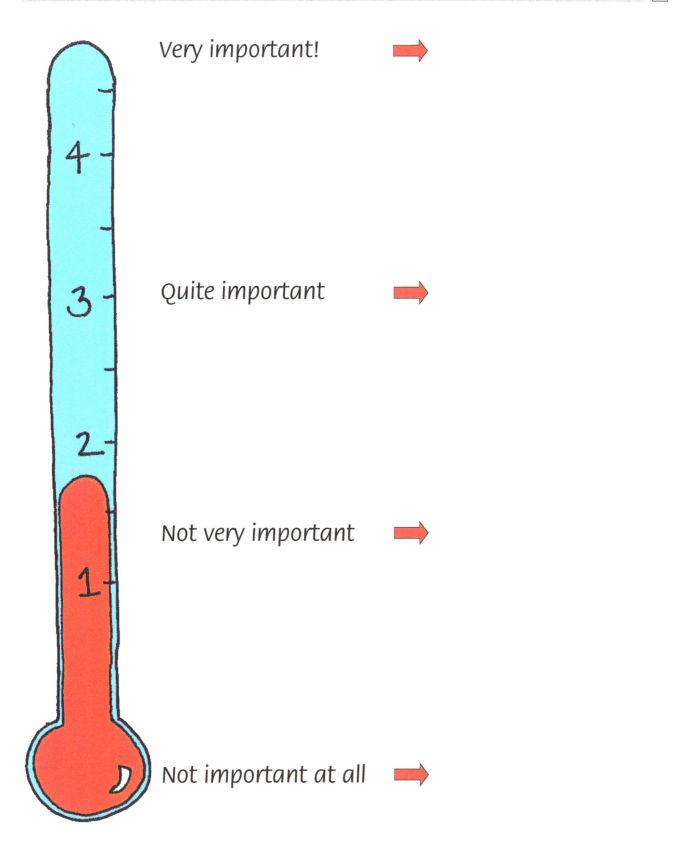

Very important! ➡

Quite important ➡

Not very important ➡

Not important at all ➡

Activity 33 Qualities of a friend

Have the latest games and gadgets	Be nice looking	Be polite
Be thoughtful	Be helpful	Be honest
Be trustworthy	Be cool and fashionable	Give compliments
Be naughty	Be good fun	Be rich

Activity 33 Qualities of a friend

Give me things	Make me laugh	Be kind and caring
Be happy	Be easy to talk to	Be a good listener
Be hardworking	Be well behaved	Be good at sharing
Be good at sports	Have similar interests	Be popular

Activity 33 Qualities of a friend

Name: ....   Date: ....

Daily Shout

Monday 14th February

Lonely hearts

Wanted, one friend.
Must...

Please contact
me soon!

Next week's issue – How to make friends and keep them. The do and don'ts in a friendship, what could you do better?

Activity 34 Qualities of a partner

Preparation

Use the qualities from Activity 33 and put them into a bag or hat.

Enlarge and print the thermometer worksheet in A3.

Print out a copy of the lonely hearts worksheet and a copy of the qualities on A4 for each group member.

Instructions

- The facilitator should explain that this week they will be exploring qualities we might look for in a potential partner.

- Group members take it in turns to pick out a quality from the bag/hat and place it on the thermometer, depending how important they feel it is.

- They should then discuss why they have chosen to place it there.

- There will be different opinions in the group, reassure the group that this is ok and discuss them.

- Group members then complete a lonely hearts worksheet, cutting and sticking their top four qualities they look for in a partner into the spaces provided.

- The group should compare their top four qualities for a friend with the qualities they have chosen for a partner. Discuss if they are the same or different and why this might be.

Introduction to relationships

Activity 34 Qualities of a partner

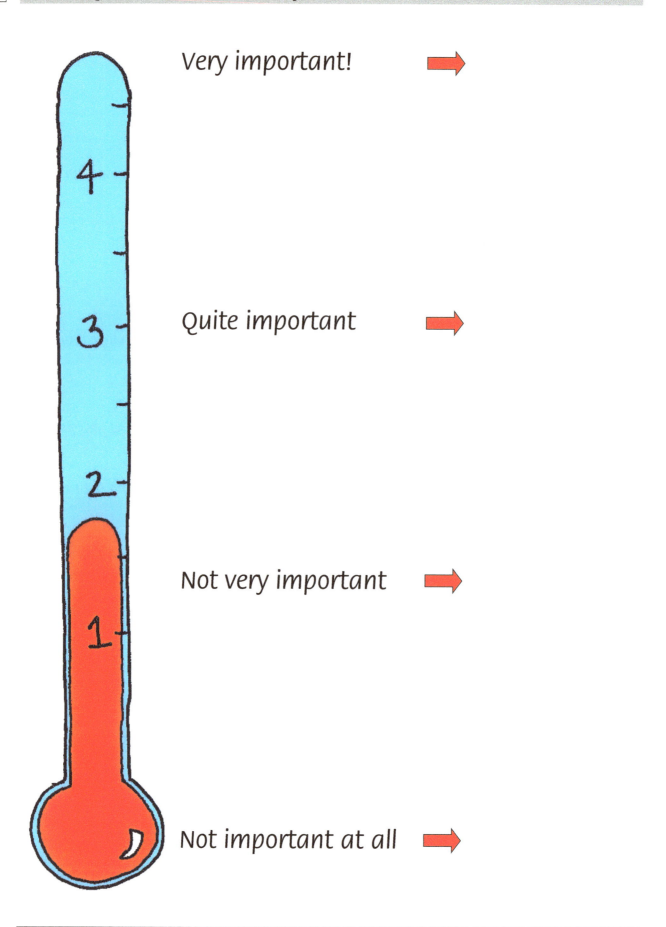

© 2017, *Talkabout Sex and Relationships*, Alex Kelly and Emily Dennis, Routledge

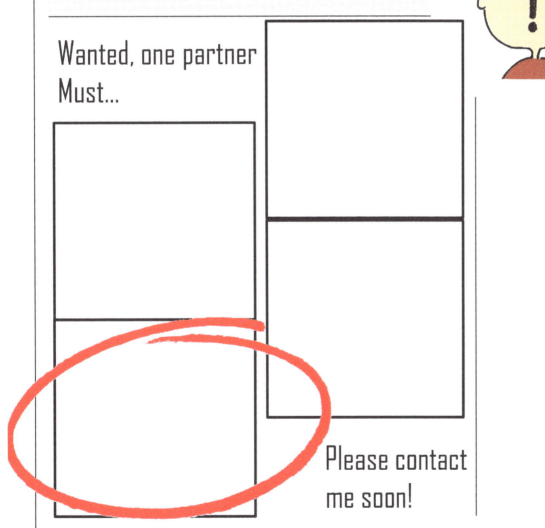

Daily Shout

Monday 14th February

Lonely hearts

Wanted, one partner
Must...

Please contact
me soon!

Next week's issue – How to find a partner and keep them. The do
and don'ts in a relationship, what could you do better?

Activity 35 What is love?

Preparation

Print the worksheets as appropriate: A4 size for individual work or A3 for group work. Alternatively you could mind map these themes on a piece of flipchart paper.

You may also wish to print out images or use pictures from magazines which people may associate with love.

Instructions

- Group members should create a poster of all the things we associate with love. This could be family, friend or relationship love.

- They should discuss what love is, are there different types of love and what does love feel like.

- The group should then decide on a definition of love to write in the box at the bottom. They can either think of their own or look it up in a dictionary or online.

Activity 35 What is love?

Name: ....   Date: ....

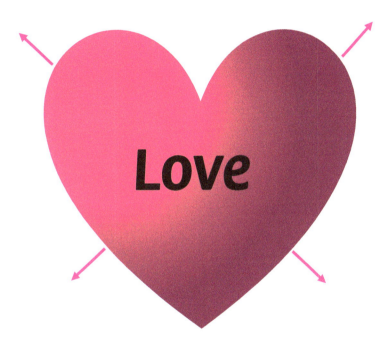

Love is...

Activity 36 Different types of love

Preparation

Print and cut out the three categories. You may wish to enlarge these to A3 and laminate if you will be using them again.

You will need the scenario cards from Activity 30 or think about a particular television programme which is regularly watched by every member of the group. You will need small pieces of paper to write the characters' names on.

Instructions

- Explain each of the three types of love, giving examples for each.

- Place the three category cards on the table in the middle of the group.

- As a group, decide on a television programme to think about (if appropriate).

- Take it in turns to either pick a scenario card from Activity 30 or think of a relationship between characters in the chosen television programme.

- Discuss if these characters share a type of love and, if so, place them under the appropriate heading.

© 2017, *Talkabout Sex and Relationships*, Alex Kelly and Emily Dennis, Routledge

Activity 36 Different types of love

Family Love

Friend Love

Relationship Love

Activity 37 What does love feel like?

Preparation

Print out a copy of the worksheet in A4 for each member of the group.

You may also need a piece of flipchart paper and pens to write down ideas.

Instructions

- Explain to the group that they will now be looking at 'relationship love' in more detail.

- The group should talk about what love feels like under the different categories. You may wish to write down ideas as a group first. You should include descriptions such as:

  1. Feelings – I feel happy when I am with this person.

  2. Thoughts – I may wonder what this person is doing even if I am not with them.

  3. Body – I can feel my heart beating faster when I am with this person.

  4. Actions – I want to do things to help this person.

- Group members should then complete their individual worksheets.

- Group members can share their ideas with the group and discuss any similarities or differences.

- Have any group members come up with idioms or metaphors such as 'butterflies in my stomach'? Discuss what these might mean.

Activity 37 What does love feel like?

Name: ....   Date: ....

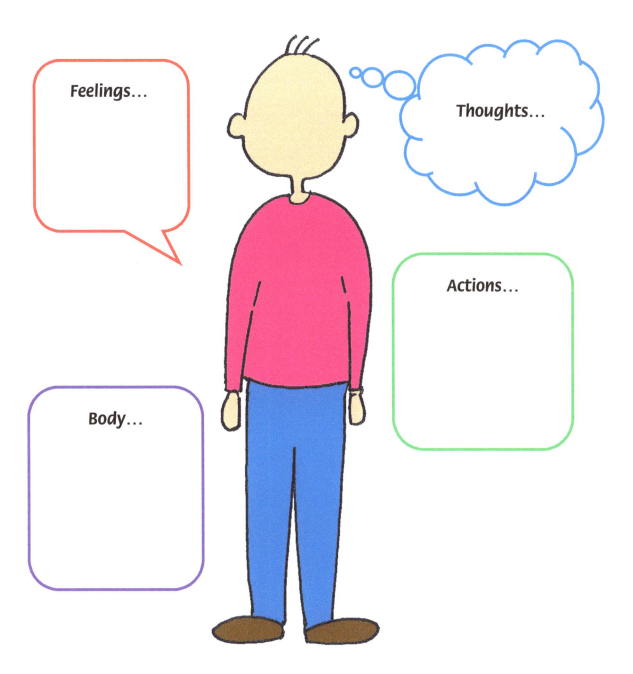

Activity 38 Romantic rhymes

Preparation

Print out a set of romantic rhymes cards. You may wish to laminate these so they can be used again.

Instructions

- Discuss the previous activity 'What does love feel like?' Did the group come up with any idioms or metaphors for love? You may wish to mind map some ideas as a group.

- This will be the focus of the session, looking at some of the well-known phrases about love and thinking about what they actually mean.

- Lay all the cards out in the middle of the group. Match the phrase and image to the definition on the romantic rhymes cards. You may wish to do this by placing the cards face down on the table and doing a 'pairs' style activity or by giving each group member a card and then they have to find the other person who has the matching card.

Variation

In pairs, research some of the other idioms or metaphors the group has thought of. Group members then feedback the definitions to the rest of the group.

Activity 38 Romantic rhymes

Weak at the knees

When you see someone you are attracted to and your body feels weak and trembles.

Butterflies in your stomach

A fluttery / bubbly feeling you get in your tummy when you are feeling nervous or excited.

Struck by cupid's arrow

A sudden, unexpected feeling of love.

Feel a spark or fireworks

A warm, excited feeling when you think of or are with someone you are attracted to. You feel happy and like nothing else matters.

Activity 38 Romantic rhymes

Chemistry

Sharing a special connection and feeling like you need to see that person again.

Head over heels

When you start having strong romantic feelings towards someone and can't think of anything else.

Fallen for someone

When you change your feelings about someone from being friends to feeling in love with them.

An old flame

Someone who you have previously been in a relationship with that you are still fond of.

Activity 39 Roll with it

Preparation

You will need two square tissue boxes. Print, laminate and Velcro™ the people and actions category cards with loop Velcro™. Place a square of hook Velcro™ on each face of the dice.

You will need the 'OK' and 'Not OK' voting cards from Activity 19.

Instructions

- The group should sit a in a circle.

- The facilitator should explain they will look at different people and different actions today then vote to indicate if we think the situation is 'OK' or 'Not OK'.

- The facilitator should attach six different actions on to one dice and six different people to the other. Start with the more familiar, less explicit cards to familiarise the group with how the activity will work.

- Swap the characters and actions then roll again.

- You may need to stick to these cards for one session then look at the more explicit actions the following session.

- Remember, when looking at partners, partners living together and a married couple, not all relationships are heterosexual.

- You may come up with some combinations that would never be ok. The group should discuss, laugh if they are comical, and move on to the next person's turn.

Activity 39 Roll with it

Mum	Dad

Brother	Sister
	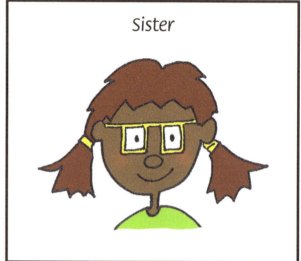
Best Friend	Partner

Activity 39 Roll with it

Grandma 	Grandad 
Male Support Worker 	Female Support Worker 
Social Worker 	Advocate 

Activity 39 Roll with it

Housemate

Neighbour

Taxi Driver

Teacher / Tutor

2+2=

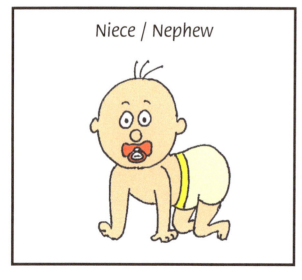

Niece / Nephew

Celebrity

Activity 39 Roll with it

Doctor

Nurse

Dentist

A stranger

Partners who live together

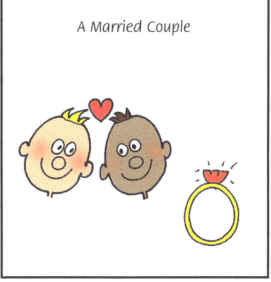

A Married Couple

Introduction to relationships

Activity 39 Roll with it

Wave	Hold Hands
	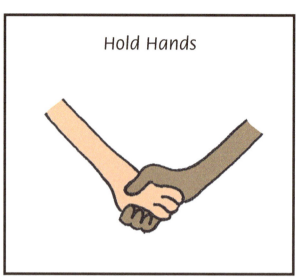
Shake Hands	Kiss cheek
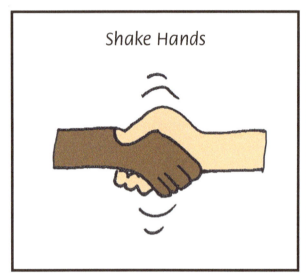	
Hug	Kiss on the Lips

Activity 39 Roll with it

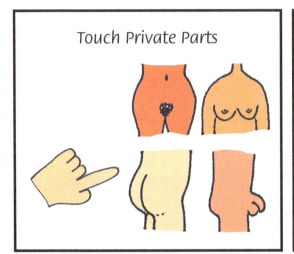
Touch Private Parts

Have Sex

Introduction to relationships

Activity 40 Mates or dates?

Preparation

This activity works well with two hoops overlapping on the floor. Place the heading cards in the hoops so it's clear which is which.

Cut out the activity cards and place them in a bag or hat. You may wish to laminate these if you will be using them again.

Alternatively, draw large yellow and red circles overlapping on a piece of flipchart paper and label with the heading cards.

Instructions

- Place the hoops overlapping on the floor in the centre of the group.

- Group members take it in turns to pick an action card and decide whether this is something friends could do, partners could do, or both.

- They then put the card in the correct place and discuss as a group. Remind the group that everyone will have different opinions and that is ok.

- If you chose to use the 'touch private parts' and 'have sex' cards, remember to discuss how long the characters have been in the relationship (e.g. if a couple started going out yesterday it may be too soon to have sex), as well as consent. Re-visit the topic of consent in Topic 2 *Staying safe* if needed.

Activity 40 Mates or dates?

Go to the cinema 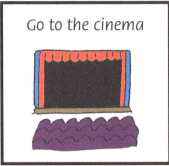	Live together 	Hug 
Kiss on the lips 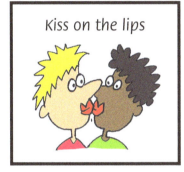	Go on holiday together 	Go out for a meal 
Get married 	Have a baby together 	Play football together 
Hold hands 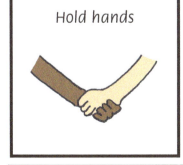	Kiss on the cheek 	High five 

 **Friends could...**

Activity 40 Mates or dates?

Go to the pub 	Go on a bike ride 	Have sleepovers 
Go for a coffee 	Chat on the phone 	Talk about worries 
Go food shopping 	Go clothes shopping 	Have a bath together 
Do their washing 	Touch private parts 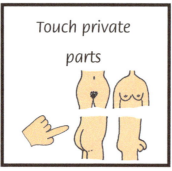	Have sex 

Partners could...

Activity 41 Relationship rules

Preparation

Worksheets should be printed out to A4 size for individual work or to A3 size for a whole group activity.

Instructions

- The group should come up with rules as to what a good relationship is.

- They should come up with the ideas themselves but the group facilitator should guide them to include the following:

  1. You must both be over 16.

  2. You must never do anything you feel uncomfortable with.

  3. You must never make a partner do anything they feel uncomfortable with.

  4. You should only have one partner at a time (a monogamous relationship).

  5. It is better to already be friends with someone before you start a relationship.

- Discuss why these rules are important.

- Group members can then place their rules into their private work folder.

 Activity 41 Relationship rules

Name: 	 Date: ....

 **Relationship Rules**

○

○

○

○

○

Remember:

Topic 4 Starting a relationship

Introduction

This topic will cover how to begin forming a relationship from choosing the right person to beginning the first conversation.

Objectives	• To introduce the concept of attraction.
	• To consider how love grows and develops over time.
	• To consider how and where you might meet new people.
	• To understand and recognise signs that someone likes you.
Materials	• Print out and laminate activities as appropriate.
	• You will need Velcro™ to make up some of the activities.
	• Print out and photocopy worksheets as appropriate.
Timing	• This topic will take up to 9 sessions to complete.

⊕ Starting a relationship

Activity	Description
What is attraction? (Activity 42)	Introduce the concept of attraction to the group. How is it different to love? The group discuss what they find attractive and decide on a definition.
Love grows (Activity 43)	The group organise and discuss the 'love grows' cards which represent the different stages of a relationship.
Perfect pair (Activity 44)	A game where the group match up different couples based on the information on the cards. Can they make a perfect pair?
Larry looks for love (Activity 45)	The group are introduced to a character called Larry. They think of places where Larry might meet a potential partner.
What should Larry say? (Activity 46)	The group explore different ways Larry could start a conversation with someone he is attracted to in the various places discussed in Activity 45.
Cupid's clues (Activity 47)	Larry meets two different women, the group read through a story and use Cupid's clues to work out if either of the women seem to be interested in him. The group decide on the best possible partner.
Fancy FACs (Activity 48)	Using the group's decision from the previous activity the group work through a FACs (feelings, actions, consequences) worksheet looking firstly at the scenario if his chosen lady says yes then if she says no.
First date phases (Activity 49)	The group look at a timeline of what happens before, during and after a first date and discuss ideas of things they could say or do at each.
Top tips for starting a relationship (Activity 50)	To end the topic, the group create their top tips for starting a relationship.

Activity 42 What is attraction?

Preparation

Print out and enlarge the worksheet to A3. Print and cut out the three definitions.

Gather images from the internet and magazines of different people (they could be celebrities) to help generate discussion.

Instructions

- Introduce the session and explain that the group will be considering a new concept today, attraction. Who has heard of it, what does it mean?

- Read out each of the three definitions.

- Group members should then vote as to which definition they think is correct for attraction. Stick the correct definition on to the worksheet.

- As a group, discuss other words we might use to describe an attraction, such as 'crush' or 'fancying someone'. Group members should add these to the definition worksheet.

- Next, place the internet/magazine images in front of the group.

- Ask group members to select an image (or a couple of images) of people they find attractive.

- Group members should then take it in turns to feedback to the group the image(s) they have chosen and why they find that person attractive. Discuss whether it is their physical appearance, personality or both which attracts you to somebody.

- Add these ideas to the worksheet.

Attraction means....

Activity 42 What is attraction?

A romantic interest, someone you find exciting, desirable and interesting. You may have romantic thoughts about them.

Enjoying spending time with someone, having a laugh and feeling happy in their company.

Enjoying seeing someone that you don't see regularly. You say "hello" when you see them but don't think about them afterwards.

Starting a relationship

Activity 43 Love grows

Preparation

Print out all the cards; these are best done in colour. To make the cards up take the left-hand picture card and stick it back to back with the right-hand question card.

These cards are best laminated as they will be used again in later activities.

Instructions

- Explain to the group that today you will be looking at how love grows and develops.

- Muddle the cards up and place them in front of the group, picture side up. Ask the group to work together and try to put the cards into the right order.

- When they think this is done, turn the cards over and swap any around that are out of place. Then, talk through the different stages of how the tree grows and what it needs.

- At each stage, refer back to how this relates to the development of love and read the questions on the card.

- If anyone in the group is in a relationship, or if one of the facilitators is and feels comfortable to talk about it, talk through each stage and relate it to how they met their partner and developed their relationship.

- Finally, ask the group which stage they think shows an initial attraction or crush, and which shows the start of love.

Activity 43 Love grows

 **Step** **1**

Choosing the seed:

What do you look for in a
partner?
What is the attraction?
Why did you choose
them?

 **Step** **2**

Do you have space?:

Do you want a
relationship right now?
Are you ready to have a
relationship?
Are you happy with who
you are?

Activity 43 Love grows

 **Step ❸**

Getting the soil:

Do you have a
foundation?
Are you already friends?
Do you spend time
together?

 **Step ❹**

Growing the seedling:

Do you spend time
together?
Do you know them well?
Do you still like them?

Activity 43 Love grows

Step 5

Established tree:

Do you know them well?

Do you trust and value
each other?

Do you care for each
other?

Step 6

Coping with problems:

Can you compromise?

Do you support each
other?

Can you overcome
problems and still love
one another?

Activity 43 Love grows

 Step **7**

A mature tree:

Do you share the same
hopes and dreams?
Can you stay together
even through difficult
times?
Are you still happy
together?

Activity 44 Perfect pair

Preparation

Print, cut out and laminate the pair cards. You could print multiple copies of the 'card backs' page to cut out and stick back to back with each of the pair cards if you wish.

Instructions

- Place pair cards in the middle of the group. Cards can be face up or face down depending on the ability of the group.

- Group members take it in turns to choose two cards and see whether or not they make a perfect pair based on the three pieces of information on the card.

- Sometimes the group may find one similarity but they should then look back and see if anyone else would be a better match (have more things in common).

- The group should continue until they think they have found a perfect match for each person.

- The group could then discuss the different pairings and why it is important to have things in common in a relationship. What matches would we look for in a relationship?

Activity 44 Perfect pair

James

- Is attracted to women
- Likes blonde hair
- Has a dog

Heidi

- Is attracted to men
- Has a dog
- Likes reading

Mo

- Is attracted to women
- Is funny
- Likes cooking

Jade

- Is attracted to men
- Likes cooking
- Likes people who make her laugh

Activity 44 Perfect pair

Chris

- Is attracted to men
- Enjoys travelling
- Has two dogs

Barry

- Is attracted to men
- Loves animals
- Loves exploring new countries

Ellen

- Is attracted to women
- Likes swimming
- Likes blue eyes

Stella

- Is attracted to men and women
- Likes brown hair
- Likes swimming

Starting a relationship

Activity 44 Perfect pair

Victor

- Is attracted to women
- Likes reading
- Loves music

Deepti

- Is attracted to men
- Loves music
- Writes books

Gemma

- Is attracted to men
- Loves pizza
- Likes kind people

Louis

- Is attracted to men and women
- Is kind
- Loves pizza

Activity 44 Perfect pair

Alisha

- Is attracted to men
- Loves swimming in the sea
- Likes beards

Gavin

- Is attracted to women
- Likes brown eyes
- Loves the beach

Karl

- Is attracted to men and women
- Loves football
- Loves films

Harriet

- Is attracted to men
- Likes going to the cinema
- Loves football

Activity 44 Perfect pair

Activity 45 Larry looks for love

Preparation

Print out a worksheet for each group member or, alternatively, cut out a number of building templates to make this a group-based activity.

Instructions

- The group facilitator reads out the 'Larry looks for love' story to the group.

- Group members should then write ideas of different locations on to the building templates for places Larry could go to meet new people. They could do this individually or discuss ideas as a group.

- Remind the group to think about any clues in the story that might give us ideas of where Larry could go to meet a potential partner.

- Group members should then feedback their ideas if they have worked individually. You could stick them all up on to a wall or large piece of paper. Discuss the pros and cons for the different places.

Activity 45 Larry looks for love

Larry…

Larry is a young man with lots of friends. He enjoys spending time with them and having fun either out and about or relaxing at home.

Larry works part time in a shop which he loves as he gets to meet and chat to lots of people. He also has lots of hobbies like football, reading and volleyball.

Although he has lots of friends Larry would also like to find love and a special person to share his life with, but he doesn't know where to start.

Help Larry to think of places where he could possibly meet someone special.

Activity 45 Larry looks for love

Name: .... Date: ....

Help Larry think of places where he could meet someone special

Activity 46 What should Larry say?

Preparation

Print and cut out the speech bubbles. You may wish to print in card and laminate the bubbles if you would like to use dry wipe pens.

Print out one prompt sheet for the group to share.

Instructions

- Choose one of the place ideas you came up with for Larry in the previous activity.

- He has seen someone there that he is attracted to and would like to start a conversation with them, but what should he say?

- Place a pile of speech bubbles in the middle of the group and take it in turns to think of possible conversation starters.

- The group could either do this verbally, with the facilitator writing down the ideas, or write their own speech bubbles.

- The group can use the prompt sheet of different starters to help generate ideas.

- The facilitator should introduce these categories and give examples for each.

- Once the group has thought of a number of ideas for conversation starters at the first location, you may wish to repeat the activity at a different location. Compare ideas, are they the same or different? Why might this be?

Activity 46 What should Larry say?

Activity 46   What should Larry say?

 Greetings

 Comment

 Questions

 Chat up lines

 Ask for something

 Something else

Activity 47 Cupid's clues

Preparation

Print and cut out the good and bad 'signs' cards.

Print out the heading cards and stick 'Good signs' at the top of one large sheet of paper and the 'Bad signs' to the top of a second piece of paper.

Print out both parts of the story and laminate if you wish to use it again.

Instructions

- Begin by asking the group how you know when someone likes you. What are the signs? Once the group have come up with a few ideas (or before if they are finding it difficult) place the large pieces of paper out in the middle of the group and the 'signs' cards face down in a pile.

- Group members take it in turns to select a card, turn it over and decide if this would be a 'good sign' that someone likes you or a 'bad sign'. Once agreed they stick the card on to the correct paper and the next person has a turn.

- Continue until all cards have been sorted.

- Next, split the group into two teams and give the 'good signs' sheet to one and the 'bad signs' sheet to the other. Each group also has a pen of the same colour e.g. they both have a blue pen.

- Explain that you are going to read the first part of the story and each group must listen out for signs on their sheet and if they hear them, circle them. After part one, discuss Rosie and whether she showed good or bad signs; which group had the most signs circled?

- Pass both groups another coloured pen.

- Repeat with part two of the story and discuss Tara's signs; were they mainly good or bad? Who showed the better signs to Larry?

✓ Good signs

Good eye contact

Laughs and smiles

Asks questions

Chatty

Have a lot in common

Suggests meeting again

Friendly posture

Shares about themselves

Activity 47 Cupid's clues

Bad signs

Looks away

Looks bored

Doesn't ask questions

Is very quiet

I'm a vegetarian

I like meat

Like different things

Fidgets

Turns away

um... er...

Difficult to talk to

Activity 47 Cupid's clues

Larry's search continues . . . part one

Larry is feeling excited. He likes the idea of meeting someone who has similar interests to him. The next week he goes to his local football ground with his friend Julian to watch his team play. They arrive and wait with the crowds to be let in. Once inside, Julian suddenly sees a woman he works with. 'Hey Rosie!' he shouts. Rosie comes over to say hello to them.

Julian introduces Larry and Rosie and then says he is just going to buy a programme and then will come back. Larry turns to Rosie who is smiling and looking at him. 'So, do you come to the football often?' he asks. Rosie nods and tells Larry that she has supported this team for ages and used to come with her dad. They continue chatting about football and also discover that they both like volleyball, reading and would both like to go to America one day.

Larry is really enjoying talking to Rosie who seems very friendly and is smiling and nodding along as they chat. He has found out a lot about her and is sad when Julian returns and suggests they go and find their seats. Rosie, who is fidgeting with her hands, says she should go to find her friend but asks if she will see Larry at the match next week. He says that he will be there and so Rosie says goodbye and that she is looking forward to seeing him again.

Activity 47 Cupid's clues

Larry's search continues . . . part two

Still feeling excited at meeting Rosie, Larry and Julian find their seats and get ready for kick off. Just as the whistle blows to begin the game, Larry can see a women squeezing down the aisle to her seat next to him. 'Hello' he says, trying to be friendly. 'Oh hi,' the woman says. 'Bit crowded today isn't it, where did you park?'

Larry is a bit surprised by her sudden question and she seems annoyed. He answers her question while she looks through her bag and doesn't turn to look at him at all. She then says that her name is Tara and that she doesn't really like football and would prefer to be gardening on a sunny Saturday. Larry asks her what else she enjoys but Tara ignores his question and instead asks him lots of questions about the football club while fidgeting with her clothes and hair. When Larry replies, Tara looks away and seems bored; a few times she doesn't even let him finish before asking her next question. In the end Larry decides to end the conversation and focus on the football match; Tara has turned to talk to the man sat on her other side anyway.

Activity 48 Fancy FACs

Preparation

Print out two copies of the FACs (Feelings, Actions, Consequences) sheet. You may also like to use coloured pens.

Instructions

- Recap on the previous session by reminding the group about Larry and the two women he met in the story. Ask them what they think he should do next. Introduce the topic of 'asking someone out' if it has not come up.

- Place one of the FACs worksheets in the centre of the group and talk the group through each of the boxes.

- Firstly get the group to think about a likely place Rosie and Larry may see each other again. Good ideas may be 'at the football the following week' or 'at Julian's house'. Add this to the sheet.

- Think about how Larry may be feeling before asking Rosie out. You could ask each group member individually or discuss together and write ideas in.

- Then think about what Larry could say. How might he ask Rosie out?

- On the first sheet, assume Rosie will say yes and fill in the two boxes for her accordingly (e.g. she is excited and says 'yes') and then the consequence.

- When you have finished completing the sheet, explain that you are going to now think about what may happen if Rosie says 'no'.

- In a different coloured pen discuss ideas of how she may be feeling if she doesn't want to go out with Larry and so what she might say when he asks her. Then add on the consequence to this.

- Discuss as a group that sometimes this will happen, sometimes people who we are attracted to won't be attracted to us or don't want a relationship and **this is ok**. Talk about how you might deal with this.

Additional activity

If the group is able, you could extend discussions by then adding Larry's feelings to Rosie saying 'yes' or 'no' and then what he may say in response, going through the middle four boxes again. You can continue this until each scenario has been explored completely.

Activity 48 Fancy FACs

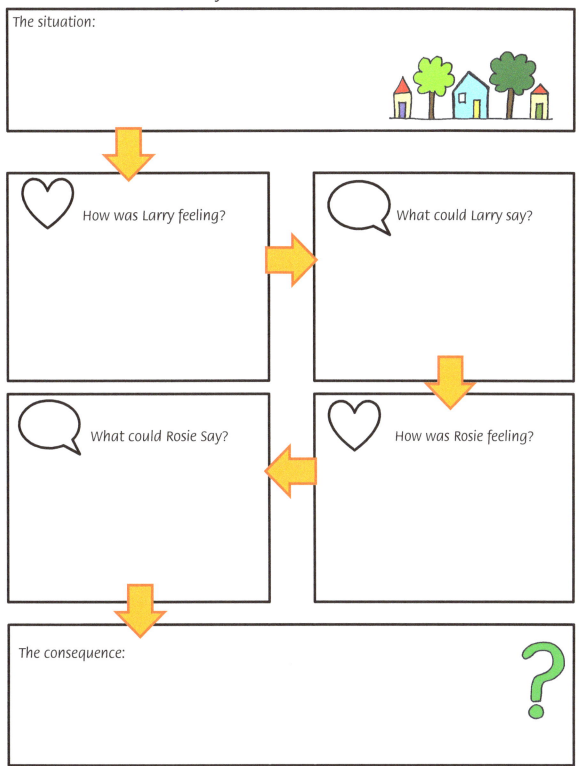

Activity 49 First date phases

Preparation

Print out the first date phases timeline and enlarge to A3.

Instructions

- Explain to the group that today they are going to be thinking about first dates. What happens and what we should do.

- Ask the group to think about the different stages of a date and place the timeline worksheet in the middle of the group.

- Introduce the timeline and talk through the stages then focus on the first stage. Ask the group how they might be feeling at this point and write this into the heart. Then talk about what you might do at this point: e.g. choose an outfit, check transport, tell someone where you are going and what time, etc.

- Continue to complete for the other three stages. Remember to think about elements such as safety, practicalities, social skills and conversations (including questions or topics). This activity may extend into a second session if you want to talk in depth about different areas such as questions or personal appearance.

Variation

If the group are able to you may like to use a large piece of paper and create the timeline on that rather than using the template. The group could then come up with the different points themselves and could also add more than shown on the worksheet, for example 'finishing a date' or break down 'before the date' into a few days before and on the day. Then as above, add in how they would feel at each stage and what they could do.

Activity 49 First date phases

The first date...

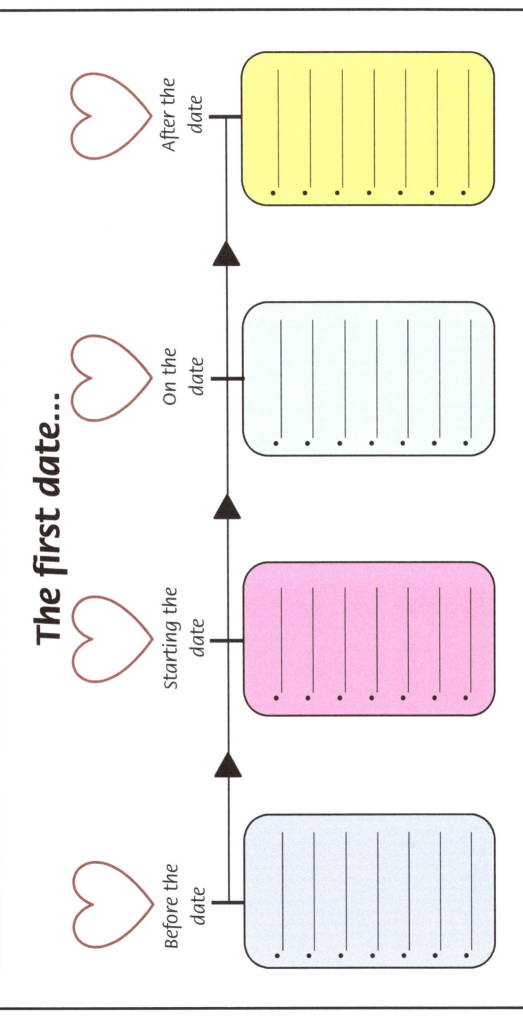

Before the date

Starting the date

On the date

After the date

Activity 50 Top tips for starting a relationship

Preparation

Worksheets should be printed out in A4 for individual work or enlarged to A3 for a whole group activity.

Instructions

- The group should come up with a list of top tips for starting a relationship, thinking about the skills practised in this topic.

- You may wish to discuss these as a group first or group members can complete the sheet individually then share ideas after.

- This sheet can then go in their individual work folders.

Activity 50 Top tips for starting a relationship

Name: ....   Date: ....

Top Tips

Do you come here often?

○

○

○

○

○

○

Remember:

📄 🧍 Topic 5 Developing a relationship

Introduction

This topic will cover how relationships begin and develop over time. It will also lead the group to recognise and explore the skills needed to have a good relationship.

Objectives
- To explore the stages of how a relationship develops.
- To understand the importance of trust in a good relationship.
- To think about how we might support a partner through good and bad situations.
- To know how to show that we value a partner.

Materials
- Print out and laminate activities as appropriate.
- You will need Velcro™ to make up some of the activities.
- Print out and photocopy worksheets as appropriate.

Timing
- This topic will take up to 6 sessions to complete.

Activity	Description
Let it grow (Activity 51)	*The group revisit the 'Love grows' cards from the previous topic and discuss what they think is needed to develop a good relationship.*
Trust obstacles (Activity 52)	*The group work in pairs to lead one another blindfolded around an obstacle course, introducing the concept of trust.*
The trusty detective (Activity 53)	*The group read about different characters and decide whether they are trustworthy or not from the behaviours they show.*
Supportive signs (Activity 54)	*The group explore how they might support a partner in both good and bad situations.*
Valuing a partner (Activity 55)	*Group members think about something they treasure and how they look after it. They then link this to how they could value a partner.*
Top tips for developing a relationship (Activity 56)	*To end the topic, the group create their top tips for developing a relationship.*

Activity 51 Let it grow

Preparation

You will need the tree cards from Activity 43.

You will also need a large sheet of paper.

Instructions

- Introduce the group to the new topic they will be focusing on for the next few sessions: developing a relationship.

- Get out the 'Love grows' cards from Activity 43 and place them on the table in the correct order. Ask the group to select the cards that show the stage of developing and maintaining a relationship (this should be cards 4 and 5 mainly).

- Ask the group how you help a tree to grow and become strong. Ideas will be to water it, make sure it has sunlight, having good roots, etc. Then ask them to think about how you grow and maintain a relationship.

- Guide the group to thinking about having good roots – knowing your partner well, supporting one another. Giving it water – complimenting, being nice and valuing one another, caring about each other and showing support. Also consider compromising and accepting each other for who you are. Write all these ideas on a large sheet of paper.

- Complete the activity by explaining that these are the skills the group are going to consider over the following sessions.

Activity 52 Trust obstacles

Preparation

In a large room, lay out a few simple obstacles such as a chair to walk around, a low step and a hoop to step through, for example.

You will also need a few blindfolds.

Instructions

• Get the group into pairs. One person in each pair puts on a blindfold. Make sure to check that people are happy to be blindfolded before you begin the task; you could ask them to shut their eyes if not.

• The person without the blindfold then has to lead their blindfolded partner safely around the obstacle course. You could ask the pairs to do a couple of laps and then switch roles so the leader is then blindfolded.

• Afterwards, talk about the activity as a group. Was it easy or hard? How did you feel with your partner? Were some parts easier than others?

• In discussions people will talk about feeling safe, knowing their partner, their partner reliably telling them what to do, staying calm and supporting them, motivating them, being caring and keeping them safe. You can then revisit the word 'trust' as these are all ways to show that you trust someone.

Activity 53 The trusty detective

Preparation

Print, cut out and laminate the trusty detective cards. You could also print multiple pages of the 'card backs' to stick on the opposite side of each card should you wish.

You will also need to print, cut out and laminate the 'Trustworthy' and 'Not trustworthy' heading cards.

Instructions

- Stick the 'Trustworthy' and 'Not trustworthy' heading cards onto opposite walls at either end of the room.

- Encourage all group members to stand up as they will be moving around for this activity.

- Read aloud the trusty detective scenario cards one at a time.

- Group members should move between the two sides of the room depending on how trustworthy they think the character is.

- If there are any differences in opinion in the group, allow discussion after each card.

- Discuss how group members would feel if these characters were their friend or partner.

- Group members should then complete the worksheet, thinking about who in their lives they trust and would talk to in different situations.

Variation

If the group would prefer to stay seated, place the pile of trusty detective cards in the centre of the circle face down; group members should then take it in turns to pick a card and sort them under the 'Trustworthy' and 'Not trustworthy' headings.

Activity 53 The trusty detective

Ellen

You and Ellen are getting ready for a party. You have bought a new top but are not sure about it so you ask Ellen for her opinion. She says she is not sure about the colour but she LOVES the top you bought last week, maybe you should wear that one instead?

Mo

You tell Mo about a surprise party you are planning for Barry. Mo works with Barry so he sees him a lot and wants to tell him about the party but manages to keep it a surprise.

Victor

You and Victor both enjoy films and often go to the cinema together. Every time you go, Victor has forgotten his wallet so you always end up paying for both of you.

Deepti

You talk to Deepti about Gemma as you are worried about her suddenly gaining weight and want to help her. Later that day, Gemma phones you in tears and asks why you have been telling everyone she is fat.

Activity 53 The trusty detective

Gavin

Gavin has forgotten his money for lunch and asks to borrow some. The next day he comes to find you and repays the money

Gemma

Gemma is going to see a band at the weekend and asks to borrow your camera. You say yes but are a little worried as it is new and very expensive. On Monday, Gemma returns the camera without any problems.

Barry

You were supposed to be meeting Barry for dinner tonight. You ring him to make sure he can still make it but he doesn't answer. Later you see photos of him on holiday abroad with his friends.

Stella

You've just had your hair cut and it is a new style which you are not sure about. You ask Stella what she thinks. She says it looks great. The next day you hear that Stella has been laughing about your new hair cut and has been telling everyone how silly you look.

Activity 53 The trusty detective

Trusty Detective

Trusty Detective

Trusty Detective

Trusty Detective

Developing a relationship

Activity 53 The trusty detective

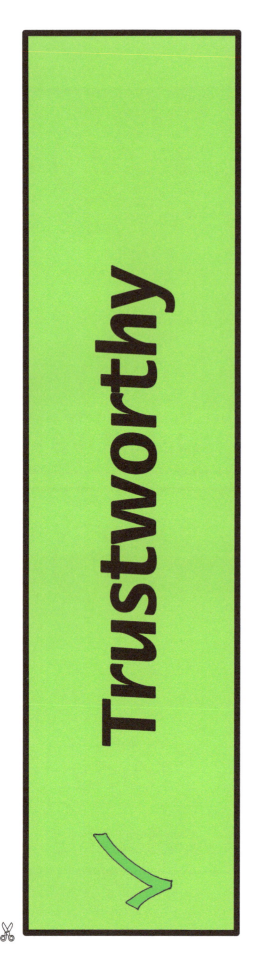

Trustworthy

Not trustworthy

Activity 53 The trusty detective

Name: ....   Date: ....

If I had a new partner, I would talk to ...

If I felt sad and low about myself, I would talk to ...

If I was worried about something personal, I would talk to ...

If I had some exciting news , I would talk to ...

Activity 54 Supportive signs

Preparation

Print, cut out and laminate the 'Supportive signs' cards.

Print out prompt sheets.

Print out worksheets in A4, one for each group member.

Instructions

- Place the supportive signs cards face down in a pile in the centre of the group.

- Group members should take it in turns to pick a card, read it aloud and think about what they could do to support a partner in that situation.

- Discuss with the rest of the group if they agree or disagree and if they have any further ideas.

- The group could use ideas from the prompt sheets if necessary.

- Once all the cards have been read out the group should then sort them into two piles: one pile of good situations and one pile of bad situations.

- Discuss whether we would support a partner in the same way for both good and bad situations. Why/why not?

- Group members could then complete the worksheet with three things they should do to support a partner in a good situation and three things they could do in a bad situation.

Activity 54 Supportive signs

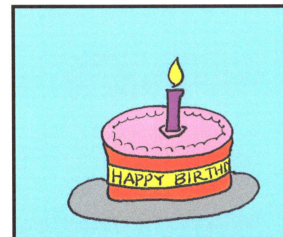

It's your partner's birthday

Your partner gets a new job

Your partner is going away with friends for the weekend

Your partner's team wins the football tournament

Developing a relationship

Activity 54 Supportive signs

Your partner buys a new laptop as theirs is broken

Your partner has an important meeting which could help them at work

Your partner loses their job

Your partner has an argument with their best friend

Activity 54 Supportive signs

Your partner is ill

Your partner has had a bad day

Your partner's dog has died

Your partner is feeling unhappy with their appearance

Activity 54 Supportive signs

Prompt sheet 1

Reassure them

Be happy and

excited for them

Be proud of them

Celebrate with them

Listen to them

Be interested

Comfort them

Give them a hug

Try to cheer them up

Activity 54 Supportive signs

Prompt sheet 2

Gossip to someone else

Offer advice

Offer to help them

Offer different ideas

Congratulate them

Ignore them

Walk away

Laugh with them

Make fun of them

Activity 54 Supportive signs

Name: .... Date: ....

When a good event happens, I could...

1.

2.

3.

When a bad event happens, I could...

1.

2.

3.

Activity 55 Valuing a partner

Preparation

You will need several large sheets of paper and coloured pens.

Print and cut out a Partner Pledge triangle for each group member.

Instructions

- Ask group members to think of something they treasure. This could be a pet or a possession but not a person.

- Now ask the group what they do to look after the thing they treasure. Encourage as many answers as possible.

- The group facilitator should write the ideas on a large piece of paper.

- Now get the group to think about what would happen to their treasured object if we don't do these things to look after it.

- The group members take it in turns to share ideas and the facilitator again should write these up.

- Now look back at the group's answers for the first question of how they look after their treasured item. Would these fit for a partner? E.g. 'give it food' – you may go for a meal together or share a pizza, 'keep it safe' – you would want to keep your partner safe, etc.

- Some may be silly so you could laugh about them or if you have a high-level group you could work out a way it may link.

- Group members could now write a pledge for one thing they will try to do to show value in their current or next relationship in one piece of the pledge bunting. If all group members complete a pledge this could be made into a string of bunting to display in the room.

Variation

Alternatively, the group could complete the 'Valuing a partner' worksheet rather than working as a group and share their ideas after.

Developing a relationship

Activity 55 Valuing a partner

Name: .... Date: ....

> Something I treasure is…
>
>

How do we look after something we treasure?	How about our relationships?
1. 2. 3.	1. 2. 3.

What happens if we don't?	What happens to our relationships?
1. 2. 3.	1. 2. 3.

Activity 55 Valuing a partner

I will try to show a partner I value them by…

I will try to show a partner I value them by…

I will try to show a partner I value them by…

Activity 56 Top tips for developing a relationship

Preparation

Worksheets should be printed out in A4 for individual work or enlarged to A3 for a whole group activity.

Instructions

- The group should come up with a list of top tips for developing a relationship, thinking about the skills practised in this topic.

- You may wish to discuss these as a group first or group members can complete the sheet individually then share ideas after.

- This sheet can then go in their individual work folders.

© 2017, *Talkabout Sex and Relationships*, Alex Kelly and Emily Dennis, Routledge

Activity 56 Top tips for developing a relationship

Name: .... Date: ....

Top Tips

○

○

○

○

○

○

Remember:

Coping with problems

 Topic 6 Coping with problems

Introduction

This topic will look at how all relationships encounter problems over time. The activities will help the group to explore what the problems are that may occur and how they might overcome them.

Objectives	• To consider the different types of problems relationships may encounter.
	• To understand the reasons why these problems might occur.
	• To discuss peer pressure and whether it is always a bad thing.
	• To discuss lying; is it always a problem?
	• To have ideas of how to cope with problems when they arise.
Materials	• Print out and laminate activities as appropriate.
	• You will need Velcro™ to make up some of the activities.
	• Print out and photocopy worksheets as appropriate.
Timing	• This topic will take up to 10 sessions to complete.

Coping with problems

Activity	Description
Problem partners (Activity 57)	The group sort scenarios into the four main problems relationships may encounter – conflict, lying, peer pressure and jealousy.
Conflicting couples (Activity 58)	The group compile a list of things couples may argue about and rate them on a scale from big to little conflicts.
Conflict – what should I do? (Activity 59)	Group members look at good and bad ideas of things to do when having an argument or conflict. They then complete a plan looking at their top three ideas.
Under pressure (Activity 60)	The group read scenarios and move between opposite sides of the room to indicate if they feel the situation is 'OK' or 'Not OK'.
Peer pressure – what should I do? (Activity 61)	Group members complete a plan of what they could do if they encountered peer pressure in a relationship.
Jealous Jamal (Activity 62)	A story is read aloud and the group list the different reasons why Jamal is feeling jealous and then discuss why.
Jealousy – what should I do? (Activity 63)	A plan is completed by each group member listing their top three ideas of things that might help them deal with jealousy in a relationship.
Little white lies (Activity 64)	Scenarios are read aloud to the group who then vote on whether they are a big lie or little lie and discuss why.
Lying – What should I do? (Activity 65)	Group members consider what they could do when dealing with lying in their own relationship. Their top three ideas are added to a worksheet.
Top tips for coping with problems (Activity 66)	To end the topic, the group create their top tips for coping with problems.

Coping with problems

Activity 57 Problem partners

Preparation

Print out the scenario cards and heading cards. Laminate if you wish to use them again.

Instructions

- Explain to the group that you are going to begin a new topic today and will be thinking about problems that might occur in a relationship and how you could cope with these.

- Have the scenario cards face down in a pile in the middle of the group. Group members take it in turns to select a card and read out the scenario.

- The group discuss what is going on in the scenario and what the problem is that is happening. **NB**: there are two scenarios around conflict, two around peer pressure, two around lying and two around jealousy.

- When you have read through and discussed all cards, place the four heading cards on the table and get the group to sort the scenarios into one of the four areas.

- Discuss the four areas; has anyone in the group ever experienced one of them in a relationship?

© 2017, *Talkabout Sex and Relationships*, Alex Kelly and Emily Dennis, Routledge

Activity 57 Problem partners

Ahmed and Lucy

Ahmed and Lucy both want a summer holiday but cannot agree on where to go. Ahmed wants to go skiing but Lucy wants to go to a hot beach. They have been talking about it for four weeks but neither will change their mind.

Tony and Roy

Tony and Roy have a dog called Rufus. Rufus needs walking. Tony says that Roy should do it as he has had a stressful day at work. Roy is annoyed and says that Tony should walk Rufus as Roy walked him yesterday and the day before and he has been at work all day too.

Lucinda and Bruce

Lucinda's new boyfriend Bruce wants to have sex but she doesn't feel ready yet. He says that everyone else is doing it and she should grow up.

Sally and Jeff

Sally and her partner Jeff have gone out for a romantic meal. Sally is having a lovely time until Jeff's friends arrive on their way to the pub. Jeff wants to go with them but Sally wants to go home. Jeff says that Sally is being stupid and boring and should stay out with them.

Activity 57 Problem partners

Steph and Leanne

Steph has finished work early and is cooking Leanne's favourite meal. Leanne is always home by 5pm but tonight is late so Steph phones her to ask where she is. Leanne apologises and says she is at the gym and will be home soon. However, Steph has just seen Leanne's trainers by the back door.

Darragh and Kelsey

Darragh has just bought himself a new games console and tells Kelsey it was second hand and only £50. A few days later Kelsey finds the receipt for the console behind the bin. It says it cost £300. Kelsey is worried as their rent is due tomorrow.

Lola and Morris

Lola and Morris have just done their final exams and get their results today. Lola is delighted as she has got top marks but Morris only just passed. Morris is surprised as he worked very hard and Lola hardly revised at all.

Chan and Anika

Anika comes home all excited as a new man has started in her office. She tells Chan all about Ricardo. Later that evening while they are watching TV Anika keeps reading her phone and giggling. When she goes to make a cup of tea Chan sees messages from Ricardo on it.

Activity 57 Problem partners

Conflict

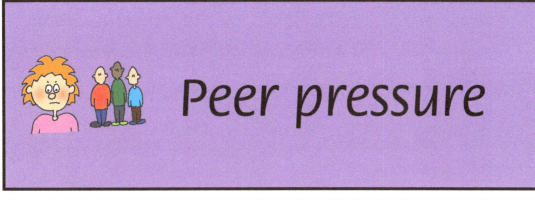

Peer pressure

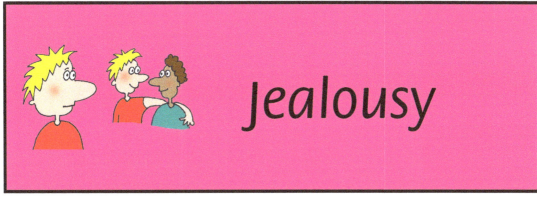

Jealousy

Lying

Activity 58 Conflicting couples

Preparation

Enlarge the conflict scale to A3. You may wish to laminate this if it will be used again.

Cut out small strips of paper for group members to write ideas on. Alternatively you could use small sticky notes.

Instructions

- Explain to the group that today they are going to talk about conflicts within a relationship. Every relationship has them from time to time.

- Begin by encouraging the group to think about all the things that couples might argue about or may have conflicting opinions over. Some ideas include: forgetting your partner's birthday, breaking their mobile phone, not spending enough time together, forgetting to buy milk, arguing about household chores or being late, etc.

- Group members should write their ideas on the strips of paper and then place them all in the centre of group.

- Group members then take it in turns to pick one up and place it where they feel is appropriate on the scale.

- They should then say why they have chosen to place it there and discuss any differences in opinion. After, the group can discuss how there are lots of different conflicts and how big they are may change how you then decide to deal with them.

Activity 58 Conflicting couples

The Conflict Scale

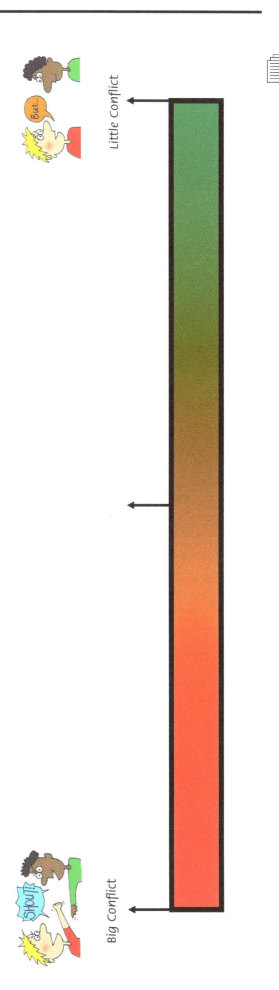

Activity 59 Conflict – what should I do?

Preparation

Print, cut out and laminate the heading and ideas cards.

A 'My plan' worksheet should be printed in A4 for each group member.

Instructions

- Re-cap on the previous session reminding the group about varying conflicts and that today you will be thinking about ideas of how to cope with these in relationships.

- Place the 'Good' and 'Bad' headings in the middle of the group and the ideas cards in a pile face down.

- Group members take it in turns to pick a card and decide whether they feel this would be a good idea or a bad idea when conflicting with a partner.

- Discuss any differences in opinion.

- Group members can add some of their own ideas to the blank cards and sort these into 'Good' and 'Bad' ideas also.

- Now group members can complete their own 'My Plan' worksheets. In the first box the group should write the situation e.g. 'If I . . . argue with my partner about the dog'.

- Get the group thinking about conflict and arguments and ask them to choose the top three ideas which they could do in conflict situations. You might like to re-read the situations discussed in the previous activity to get them started.

- They should cut and stick ideas or write them in.

- They can then complete the 'This will mean. . .' box at the end thinking about the effects these strategies might have.

Activity 59 Conflict – what should I do?

✓	**Good ideas**

✗	**Bad ideas**

 Listen to them	 Talk to them	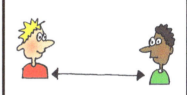 Give them space
 Compromise	 Give your reasons	 Apologise
		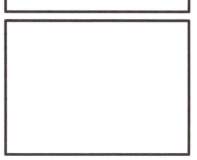

© 2017, *Talkabout Sex and Relationships*, Alex Kelly and Emily Dennis, Routledge

Name: .... Date: ....

My Plan

If I ...

I will try to...

1.

2.

3.

This will mean...

Activity 60 Under pressure

Preparation

Print out the OK/Not OK heading cards and sentence cards. Laminate if you wish to use them all again.

Print out the worksheet and enlarge to A3.

Instructions

- Introduce the session and explain to the group that they will be considering peer pressure in relationships today.

- Discuss with the group the meaning of peer pressure; have people heard it before? Can anyone think of any examples?

- Stick the OK/Not OK heading cards onto opposite walls of the room.

- The facilitator then reads out a sentence and the group move to whichever side of the room they think fits, i.e. if they think the sentence/pressure is 'OK' they quickly move towards that side.

- Continue until all cards have been explored.

- The group then come back into a circle and look at the worksheet. Firstly, they should think about the question 'Is peer pressure always bad?' and add some ideas onto the sheet.

- Next the group consider how you know when a pressure is 'good' or 'bad' and again add ideas onto the worksheet.

Variation

Instead of the group running to different sides of the room to vote whether sentences are 'OK' or 'Not OK', they could stay seated in a circle and use their voting sticks from Activity 19.

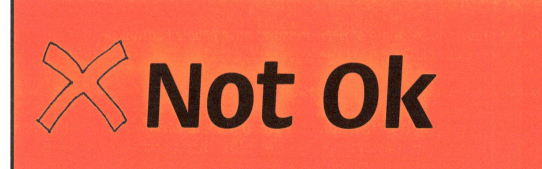

Your partner wants you to eat out every night because his colleagues do but you can't afford it.

You work hard and save money. You've been stressed at work so your partner suggests a weekend away.

Activity 60 Under pressure

Your partner keeps asking you to revise so that you will pass your exam.

Your partner likes to go to the pub every Saturday and says you are boring if you don't want to go.

Your partner wants you to try skiing on holiday as they think you will like it.

Your partner only likes you to wear clothes they have chosen and says you look ugly if you don't.

You have had lots of tooth problems and your partner keeps telling you to stop drinking fizzy drinks.

Your partner keeps asking you to touch their private parts in public. They get angry when you say no.

Activity 60 Under pressure

Name: ....   Date: ....

Is peer pressure always bad?

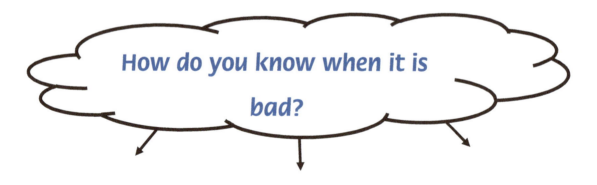

How do you know when it is

bad?

Activity 61 Peer pressure – what should I do?

Preparation

You will need the sentence cards and worksheet from Activity 60 and the 'good ideas' cards from Activity 59.

You will need an A4 'My plan' worksheet from Activity 59 for each group member as well.

Instructions

- Begin by re-capping on pressure in a relationship using the sentence cards from the previous session.

- Group members take it in turns to select a card and read the sentence. They then think of one thing that you could do in that situation. Continue until all cards have been discussed.

- The group then each complete a 'My plan' worksheet for peer pressure. You could lay out the 'good ideas' cards from Activity 59 to help the group generate ideas.

- If the group are able to, when they choose a coping strategy such as 'Say how I feel' they could draft a sentence next to the box about how they would say/do this.

- The group could then share their ideas.

Coping with problems

Activity 62 Jealous Jamal

Preparation

Print out the story and laminate if you wish to use it again.

You will need a few large sheets of paper and a pen.

You may also like to use the 'OK' and 'Not OK' voting cards from Activity 19.

Instructions

- Explain to the group that you are going to be thinking about a new topic today, the topic of jealousy. Ask the group if they know what jealousy means. Write ideas on a piece of paper.

- Read the story to the group. You might like to read it once and then read it again asking the group to think about what things were making Jamal feel upset and jealous.

- Make a list on a large sheet of paper as a group of all the things that are making Jamal jealous in the story and why.

- Next go through each one and ask if it is 'ok' for him to feel jealous about that or not. The group could vote using their cards from Activity 19, or draw a tick or a cross by the ideas on the sheet of paper.

© 2017, *Talkabout Sex and Relationships*, Alex Kelly and Emily Dennis, Routledge

Activity 62 Jealous Jamal

Jamal and Leticia

Jamal and Leticia have been together for three years and are really happy. They love spending time together and have lots of hobbies they both enjoy doing like rock climbing and walking.

Lately though Jamal has been feeling upset and that things have not been going his way. He has been working hard in his job as he could get a promotion and a pay rise soon. Leticia has just started a new job and within two weeks was given a big promotion meaning she now manages her team. Jamal is happy for her but also feels more pressure now to get his promotion too.

That evening Leticia comes home and tells Jamal her good news, she also suggests they go for a walk. Jamal agrees as it's a lovely evening but then notices Leticia is wearing brand new trainers.

Activity 62 Jealous Jamal

When he asks her about them she says she bought them after work to celebrate. Jamal looks at his dirty old trainers with holes in them. He would like new trainers too but can't really afford them right now.

On their walk Jamal begins to cheer up as they chat about different things including their plans for the next few weekends. They might try climbing at a new centre or take their friend's dog to the beach. Leticia then remembers that actually next weekend she has promised to go away with her friends for a shopping weekend. Jamal is happy that she spends time with her friends but she is always shopping and seeing other people meaning they have less and less time to spend together as a couple. He has also has been trying to set up a date to go to the football with his friends but they are always busy.

Feeling more and more gloomy, Jamal and Leticia begin their walk back home. As they turn the last corner Leticia spots something blowing around on the pavement in front of them. She stops to pick it up and sees it is a scratch card that someone has dropped. She looks around and there is no one else on the street. 'Go on, scratch it and see,' says Jamal, trying hard to put on a smile. Leticia does and then turns to Jamal looking shocked. 'I think I have won £200!' she shouts. She is so excited, Jamal hugs her and says how pleased he is and isn't she lucky. 'What will you spend it on?' he asks. Leticia says she thinks she will give it to her mum as she has been feeling sad recently and could do with a few new things like a kettle and some shoes as her favourite pair have a hole. 'Oh,' Jamal says. 'That's nice.'

Activity 63 Jealousy – what should I do?

Preparation

You will need an A4 copy of the 'My plan' worksheet for each person and the 'good ideas' cards from Activity 59.

Instructions

- Begin by re-capping on jealousy in a relationship by asking if anyone in the group has ever felt jealous of a partner and if they would like to, share why.

- The group then each complete a 'My plan' worksheet for jealousy. You could lay out the 'good ideas' cards from Activity 59 to help the group members generate ideas.

- If the group are able to, when they choose a coping strategy such as 'Say how I feel' they could draft a sentence of what they might say next to the box.

- The group could then share their ideas.

Activity 64 Little white lies

Preparation

Print and enlarge the 'All lies are bad' mind map to A3.

Print, laminate and attach the 'Big lie'/'Little lie' cards to lollypop sticks to use as voting cards for the group. You will need to make enough so each group member has a pair.

Print and cut out the lie cards. Laminate these if you wish to use them again.

Instructions

• Introduce the concept of lying to the group; do they all know what it means? Has anyone got an example of a lie they have heard?

• Discuss the phrase 'All lies are bad', what do group members think? Is this always the case or can, on occasion, lies be OK? Write ideas onto the worksheet.

• Ask the group what a 'white lie' is and discuss people's definitions.

• Hand out the 'Big lie'/'Little lie' voting sticks to each group member and place the 'lie cards' face down in a pile in the centre of the group.

• Take it in turns to select a card and read out the lie.

• Group members then vote on whether they think this is a 'big lie' or a 'little lie'.

• Discuss any differences of opinion in the group.

© 2017, *Talkabout Sex and Relationships*, Alex Kelly and Emily Dennis, Routledge

Activity 64 Little white lies

Activity 64 Little white lies

Little Lie	**Big Lie**
Little Lie	**Big Lie**
Little Lie	**Big Lie**

Activity 64 Little white lies

Your partner tells you they can't afford to go to the cinema but then go with a friend the next day.	You cook a meal for your partner. They don't like it but just tell you they have already eaten.
Your partner borrows your car and scratches it on a bush. When you ask, they say they have no idea how it got there.	You and your partner are on your way back from a karaoke party. You ask if your terrible singing was ok. They say it was perfect.
Your family are having a big party today. Your partner doesn't like them so tells you they are feeling ill and can't go with you.	You wake up with a big spot on your nose and are upset. Your partner says it doesn't look bad and no one will notice.
You tell your partner a secret. They tell a friend and when you ask if they have told anyone, they say "No, of course not!".	You ask how your partner's day has been. They are tired, fed up and don't want to talk about it so say it was OK.

Activity 65 Lying – what should I do?

Preparation

You will need the eight 'lie cards' from Activity 64.

You will need the worksheet and 'good ideas' cards from Activity 59.

Instructions

- Begin by re-capping on lying in a relationship by looking back at the eight lie cards from Activity 64. Group members take it in turns to read a card and say one thing they might do in that situation.

- The group then each complete a 'My plan' worksheet for lying. You could lay out the 'good ideas' cards from Activity 59 to help the group generate ideas.

- If the group are able to, when they choose a coping strategy such as 'Say how I feel' they could draft a sentence of what they might say next to the box.

- The group could then share their ideas.

Activity 66 Top tips for coping with problems

Preparation

Worksheets should be printed out in A4 for individual work or enlarged to A3 for a whole group activity.

Instructions

- The group should come up with a list of top tips for coping with problems, thinking about the skills practised in this topic.

- Encourage the group to think about the areas covered; conflict, peer pressure, jealousy and lying. The group might like to also get out their 'My Plan' worksheets for ideas.

- You may wish to discuss these as a group first or group members can complete the sheet individually then share ideas after.

- This sheet can then go in their individual work folders.

Name: ....   Date: ....

Top Tips

○

○

○

○

○

○

Remember:

Topic 7 When a relationship ends

Introduction

This topic looks at the issue of when a relationship ends. Not all relationships last and they may end for many reasons. It will also cover how we can cope with this, what we can do to make us feel better and that we can be happy without a relationship too.

Objectives	• To consider why a relationship may end.
	• To have a few ideas of what we can do to make ourselves feel better.
	• To know what else in our lives makes us happy.
	• To discover the positives and negatives of being in a relationship.
	• To consider the positives and negatives of being single.
Materials	• Print out and laminate activities as needed.
	• You may need Velcro™ to make up some of the activities.
	• Print out and photocopy worksheets as appropriate.
Timing	• This topic will take up to 7 sessions to complete.

When a relationship ends

Activity	Description
Why might a relationship end? (Activity 67)	The group read and sort scenarios into different reasons why a relationship might end to introduce the topic.
Emotional endings (Activity 68)	Using the scenarios from the previous activity, the group look at a worksheet considering how each partner might feel when a relationship ends.
Coping strategies (Activity 69)	Group members discuss ideas of what they could do if a pet or plant died then link this to what they could do if their relationship ended.
Heartbroken Henry (Activity 70)	The group look at a character called Henry who has just split up with his girlfriend. They consider how Henry might feel and ideas of what he could do at different stages to help him feel better.
See-saw of love (Activity 71)	The group sort cards showing positives and negatives of being in a relationship or being single. They discuss that one is not better than the other.
Loving life (Activity 72)	Sheets are completed by each group member thinking about all the things in their lives that make them happy.
Top tips for a relationship ending (Activity 73)	To end the topic, the group create their top tips for when a relationship ends.

Activity 67 Why might a relationship end?

Preparation

Print and cut out the scenario and heading/category cards. Stick them back to back and then laminate if you wish to use them again. On the sheet the cards are arranged so you can stick the left card back to back with the right card.

Enlarge the worksheet to A3.

Instructions

- Explain to the group that you are going to begin a new topic today and will be thinking about why a relationship may end.

- Have the scenario cards in a pile in the middle of the group, story side up. Group members then take it in turns to select a card and read out the scenario without letting the group see the back/category.

- The group discuss what is going on in the scenario and why it may cause the relationship to end. When they think they have decided they turn the card over to see if they are right.

- You could then place the card, category side up, on to the worksheet.

Additional activity

The group could come up with different ideas of why couples may end their relationships under the different category headings.

Activity 67 Why might a relationship end?

You have been with your partner for six years and get on very well. Your partner has just been offered their dream job in Dubai. You don't want to leave as your family, friends and job are here.

Distance

Your partner tells you that they are very sorry but they aren't in love with you anymore. They say that they would like to stay friends but there just isn't that 'spark' anymore.

Falling out of love

(One person)

You and your partner sit down for an open and honest discussion. You both feel like you have been growing apart from some time and are no longer in love.

Falling out of love
(Both people)

Activity 67 Why might a relationship end?

You and your partner are chatting about the things you want in life. You really want to settle down, get married and have a family. They do not want this, they want to travel the world and experience new things.

Wanting different things

Your partner tells you that they are very sorry but they are now in love with someone else. They want to be with that person instead.

Cheating

Your partner has been spending £30 a week on French lessons for the last year. You have just found out that they have never been and have been spending all the time and money at the pub.

Lying

When a relationship ends

You and your partner argue constantly, you don't seem to agree about anything. Even when you try to spend quality time together you end up disagreeing and shouting at each other.

Arguments

You feel very unhappy in your relationship. Your partner is always rude to you and makes you feel like you are not good enough.

Unhappiness

You and your partner have had a difficult year. Your partner lost their job and can't find another one. This means you now have two jobs and never get a rest. It has put a lot of strain on the relationship.

Stress

Activity 67 Why might a relationship end?

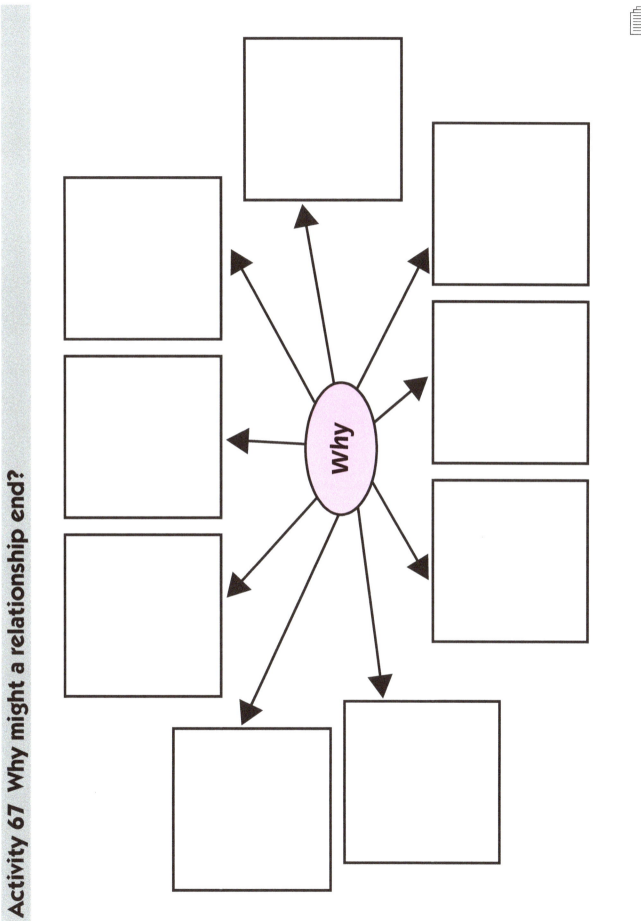

When a relationship ends

Activity 68 Emotional endings

Preparation

Print out and enlarge the worksheet to A3. You may like to laminate the worksheet so it can be written on with dry wipe pens and reused.

You will also need the scenario cards from Activity 67.

You may wish use a piece of flipchart paper for the word shower.

Instructions

- Begin by getting the group to generate a word shower of different emotions, writing all their ideas on a piece of paper.

- Group members then take it in turns to pick a scenario card from the previous activity and read the card out loud to the group.

- Group members should think about the different emotions associated with that situation.

- Ask the group how they might feel if this situation happened to them. Use the word shower the group made earlier to help with ideas.

- Now think about how the other person/your partner may feel in this situation. It is normal for people to feel differently about situations.

- Discuss any similarities and differences. Why might one person in the relationship feel better about the situation than the other?

© 2017, *Talkabout Sex and Relationships*, Alex Kelly and Emily Dennis, Routledge

Activity 68 Emotional endings

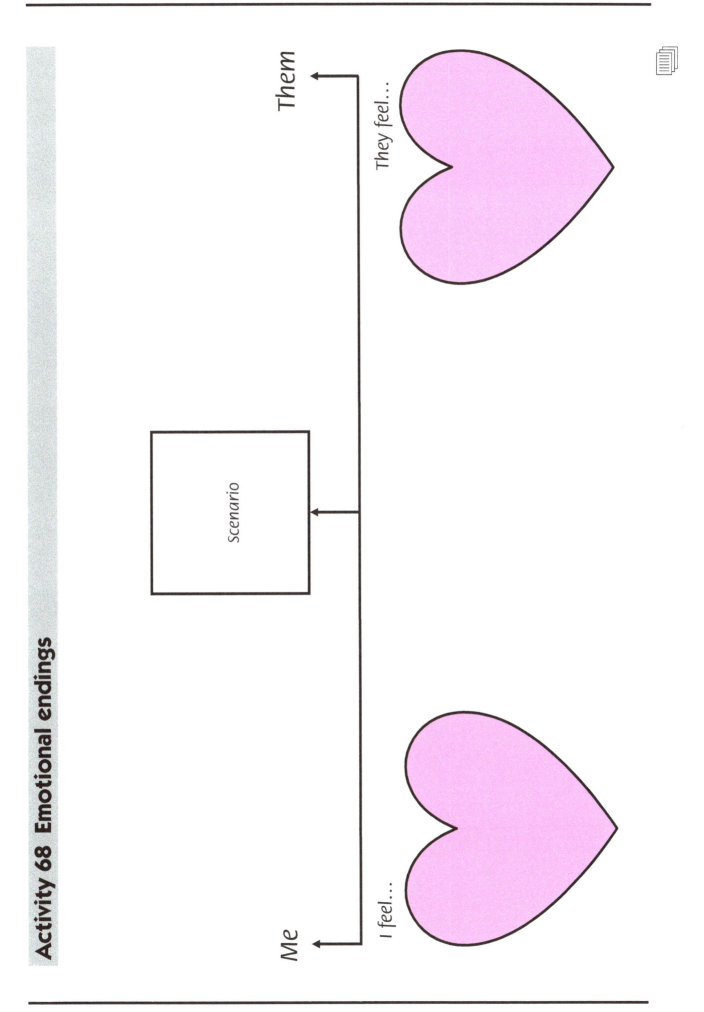

Them

They feel...

Scenario

Me

I feel...

When a relationship ends

Activity 69 Coping strategies

Preparation

Print the 'What would I do. . .?' worksheets in A4 for individual use or enlarge to A3 for group work.

Each group member will need an A4 copy of the 'My top 3' worksheet.

Instructions

- Introduce the session by saying that today you will think about when other things end and how you cope. Ask the group to think about what they might do if a pet or plant died. Write their ideas on to the worksheets.

- Then ask the group how these ideas will help the situation.

- Now ask them to think about what they might do if their relationship ended and add ideas to that worksheet.

- Compare this to the pet and plant worksheets. Are there any similarities?

- Group members could then complete the worksheet deciding on their top three ideas of what they could do if their relationship ended. Discuss as a group how these positive actions might help the situation and add this at the section at the bottom.

Possible ideas

Talk to someone	Make plans/goals	Hug friends/family
Spend time with friends	Play sport	Get rid of objects
Do activities you enjoy	Look after yourself	Say how you feel
Make new friends	Give yourself time	
Go on holiday	Distance	

Activity 69 Coping strategies

Name: .... Date: ....

What would I do if a pet died?

Activity 69 Coping strategies

Name: .... Date: ....

What would I do if a plant died?

Activity 69 Coping strategies

Name: .... Date: ....

What would I do if my relationship ended?

Activity 69 Coping strategies

Name: ....   Date: ....

My Top 3

If my relationship ended

I would try to...

1.

2.

3.

This will mean...

Activity 70 Heartbroken Henry

Preparation

Print the worksheet in A4 for individual use or enlarge to A3 for group work.

You may also need the word shower of emotions from Activity 68 and worksheets from Activity 69 to help the group generate ideas.

Instructions

- Introduce the session and tell the group that they will be thinking about a character called Henry who has just split up with his girlfriend.

- Read through the first story. Discuss as a group how Henry might be feeling on day 1. You may wish to look at ideas from the word shower of emotions. Group members can add one or a couple of emotions to the heart shape under this section.

- Now discuss as a group what Henry could do to feel better. Refer back to the worksheets from Activity 69 for ideas. Group members can add these to the box 'Henry could. . .'

- Continue with the second section. Discuss how Henry is feeling a week on and add ideas of what he could do. Think about how this has changed from the previous section and why.

- Now look at how Henry is feeling a month on from the break up, and think about things he could be doing now. How have things changed for Henry?

- Discuss as a group that relationships may end and you may feel terrible when it happens; however it does get easier and there are lots of things we can do to help ourselves feel better.

Activity 70 Heartbroken Henry

Name: ....   Date: ....

Henry and his girlfriend Henrietta have just split up. They were together for two years but were arguing a lot and just didn't get on as well as they used to.

Day 1...
Henry could…

Henry has been single for a week now. He has been trying hard to keep busy but still thinks about Henrietta a lot.

1 week...
Henry could…

It has been a month since Henry and Henrietta split up. Henry is starting to feel more like his old self again but still misses Henrietta at times.

1 month...
Henry could…

Activity 71 See-saw of love

Preparation

Print and cut out all the pro and con cards.

Print the worksheet and enlarge to A3. You may wish to laminate the worksheet and cut out the scales, adding a split pin so the scales can move up or down with different pros and cons.

Instructions

- Explain to the group that today you will be looking at the pros and cons of being in a relationship and of being single.

- Firstly, display the see-saw sheet either on the floor with the group sitting around it or on the table in the centre of the group.

- The group will now consider the pros and cons of being in a relationship. You will require the blue cards for this exercise.

- Place the cards face down in the centre of the group.

- Group members take it in turns to pick a card and decide whether they think it is a pro (good thing) or con (bad thing) and then place the card on the appropriate end of the see-saw.

- For some people, the cards may not apply. For example, if a group member dislikes touch then having someone to hug would be a bad thing. It is important to discuss individual differences and reinforce that this is ok.

- There are also blank cards for the group to add their own ideas.

- Once all the cards have been used take a look at the see-saw; what do the group notice? Which side has more or are they the same?

- Now repeat the exercise using the pink cards and discussing the pros and cons of being single.

- The see-saws should show there can be little difference, and therefore one is not necessarily better than the other.

Variation

Alternatively, group members could write ideas on to a sticker, stick these to ping pong balls or similar and add them to two glass jars, clearly demonstrating the pros and cons.

When a relationship ends

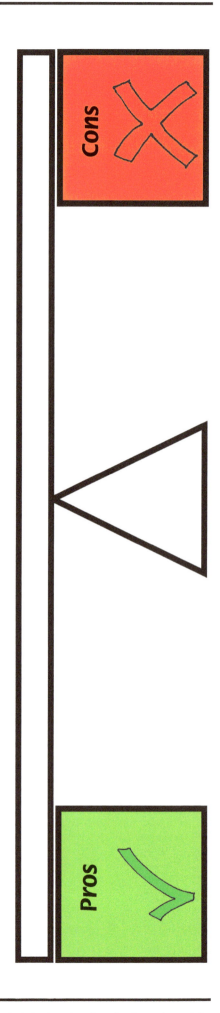

Cons

Pros

Activity 71 See-saw of love

You would have company

You could help each other

You might get more presents

You would have someone to
talk to

You would have someone to
listen to you

You would have someone to
love

You would comfort each other

You would feel more secure

Activity 71 See-saw of love

You would have someone to
laugh with

You might have arguments

You might not see your friends
as much

You might worry about them

You might feel jealous of your
partner

You might split up and feel
heartbroken

You might have less time to
yourself

You will have to compromise
and sometimes do things you
don't want to

© 2017, *Talkabout Sex and Relationships*, Alex Kelly and Emily Dennis, Routledge

Activity 71 See-saw of love

You might disagree about things

You might miss them when they are not there

You will be independent

You can do what you want when you want

You are free

You can spend lots of time with your friends

You don't have to worry about a partner

More opportunities to make new friends

Activity 71 See-saw of love

You might feel lonely

People might ask why you are still single

You might feel jealous of your friends having partners

You might feel unloved

You might feel you have no one to talk to

You might have no one to hug

Activity 72 Loving life

Preparation

Print out a copy of the worksheet and enlarge to A3 for each group member.

You may wish to provide a selection of images from magazines or the internet or ask people to bring in photographs of things which make them happy.

Instructions

- Explain to the group that you are going to be thinking about all the things that make them happy in their lives.

- You may wish to start the session with an activity like 'change places if. . .' but change the wording to 'I am happy when. . .' Group members take it in turns to call out 'I am happy when . . . I am at the beach'; they then changes places with anyone else who also feels happy at the beach and so on.

- Group members will then fill their worksheets with all the things that make them happy in their lives using words and images. Some ideas might be: family, friends, job, pets, holidays, activities, home, shopping, car, sunshine, etc.

- Relationships may come up in these ideas; discuss how relationships would only be one part of our lives, we have lots of other things that make us happy too.

- End the session with each group member saying one great thing about themselves.

Activity 72 Loving life

Name: .... Date: ....

Activity 73 Top tips for a relationship ending

Preparation

Worksheets should be printed out in A4 for individual work or enlarged to A3 for a whole group activity.

Instructions

- The group should come up with a list of top tips for when a relationship ends, thinking about the skills practised in this topic.

- Group members should consider what they can do to cope and get through this time.

- You may wish to discuss ideas as a group first or group members can complete the sheet individually then share their tips after.

- This sheet can then go in their individual work folders.

Activity 73 Top tips for a relationship ending

Name: .... Date: ....

Top Tips

○

○

○

○

○

○

Remember:

Topic 8 Looking to the future

Introduction

In this topic we will be looking at our hopes and dreams for the future, whether this is as an individual or as a couple.

Objectives	• To explore the group members' hopes, dreams and wishes for the future.
	• To consider how we might compromise if our wishes were different to those of a partner.
	• To look at and think about how we may achieve our goals.
	• To celebrate completing the course.
Materials	• Print out and laminate activities as appropriate.
	• You will need Velcro™ to make up some of the activities.
	• Print out and photocopy worksheets as appropriate.
Timing	• This topic will take up to 7 sessions to complete.

Looking to the future

Activity	Description
In full bloom (Activity 74)	The group members focus on the mature tree from the 'Love grows' activity and think about what this represents in terms of a relationship.
Wonderful wishes (Activity 75)	Group members think about what their hopes and dreams are for the future.
I have a dream (Activity 76)	Group members compare the dreams of two characters, Sarah and Steve, and link those that match and think about those that don't.
Compromising couples (Activity 77)	The group members consider what happens if our hopes and dreams for the future don't match those of our partner. Is compromise always possible?
Just around the river bend (Activity 78)	Group members complete the river worksheet adding their dreams to the trees, considering what it would take for us to achieve these.
Top tips for looking to the future (Activity 79)	To end the topic, the group members create their top tips for looking to the future.
Certificates (Activity 80)	Group members receive a certificate of achievement for completing the course.

Activity 74 In full bloom

Preparation

You will need the 'Love grows' cards from Activity 43.

You will need a piece of flipchart paper and some pens to write down ideas.

Instructions

- Explain to the group that you are going to begin a new topic today and will be thinking about their hopes and dreams for the future.

- Ask the group to have a look through the 'Love grows' cards and find the tree that corresponds with this new topic. This should be step 7 – a mature tree.

- As a group, think about a mature tree, what this means and then think about how this relates to a relationship. You could write ideas on a piece of flipchart paper. Ideas could include the tree has been standing for a long time with deep roots (long-term relationship), it has weathered difficult times but still survived (coping with problems in relationships) and it is now bearing fruit (this could represent dreams for the future).

Looking to the future

Preparation

Print and cut out several pages of wish bubbles.

You will need a top three wishes worksheet for each group member.

Instructions

- Introduce the session and explain to the group that you are going to explore their wishes and hopes for the future.

- Place the pile of wish bubbles on the table in the centre of the group.

- Group members take it in turns to write a wish on to a bubble (or draw a picture if they prefer) and share this with the group.

- Group members could then complete individual worksheets looking at their top three dreams for the future.

- They may wish to share these with the group and discuss the similarities and differences.

Activity 75 Wonderful wishes

Looking to the future

Activity 75 Wonderful wishes

Name: ....

Date: ....

Activity 76 I have a dream

Preparation

Print the worksheets in A4 for individual use or enlarge to A3 for group work.

You may wish to laminate the worksheet so it can be written on with dry wipe pens and reused.

You will also need a piece of flipchart paper and pens.

Instructions

- Introduce the session by explaining that you will continue to think about wishes and dreams for the future but also the wishes of your partner.
- Begin by discussing how you would find out what your partner wants in life and what their hopes are; what could you ask or say? When would be a good time to ask? Write down ideas on a piece of flipchart paper.
- Next, hand out the worksheet either one per person or place a large copy in the middle of the group if working together.
- Read out Sarah and Steve's wishes.
- Group members can then match up the dreams and wishes that are the same by drawing a line between them.
- Are there any that don't match up?
- Discuss with the group whether it matters if these wishes are not exactly the same; what could you do?

Activity 76 I have a dream

Name: ....

Date: ....

Activity 77 Compromising couples

Preparation

Print the worksheets in A4 for individual use or enlarge to A3 for group work.

You may wish to laminate the worksheet so it can be written on with dry wipe pens and reused.

Instructions

- Discuss with the group how we all have our own dreams and wishes for the future. We may be lucky and share some of the same wishes as our partner but it is unlikely that every wish will be exactly the same. This is where compromise comes in.

- Discuss with the group what compromise means, for example finding a solution that you are both happy with. You may wish to write a definition as a group.

- Refer back to Activity 76: Sarah and Steve share a number of dreams and wishes but some are different.

- Complete the worksheet by looking at how we could find a compromise for some of the different wishes. Start by adding Sarah and Steve's different dreams from Activity 76; the group could then add some of their own.

- Discuss how some compromises are simpler than others. For some things, such as one person wanting to have children and the other person not, you may not be able to compromise and may need to ask yourself if this relationship is right for you. For others it might be quite simple to find a fair solution.

- Depending on the level of the group you may go into more or less detail in this area, for example, if you cannot compromise then what should you do? Group members should write ideas at the bottom of the worksheet.

Looking to the future

Activity 77 Compromising couples

Name: ....

Date: ....

I want...					
We could...					
They want...					

What could we do if we don't agree?

278

© 2017, *Talkabout Sex and Relationships*, Alex Kelly and Emily Dennis, Routledge

Activity 78 Just around the river bend

Preparation

You will need to enlarge the river worksheet to A3 for each group member.

Instructions

- Hand out a copy of the worksheet to each group member.

- Group members should decide on and fill in five hopes for the future, one in each tree. You could refer back to Activity 75 for ideas if needed.

- Group members should look at their wishes and consider how they might achieve them and what might be a challenge or obstacle along the way.

- Discuss as a group how you could overcome some of these challenges. Some of the solutions may be linked into how you can overcome it as a couple, if you are in a relationship, or individually if you are on your own.

- Group members should write ideas at the bottom of the worksheet. The group could then decorate their sheets.

Activity 78 Just around the river bend

Name: ....

Date: ....

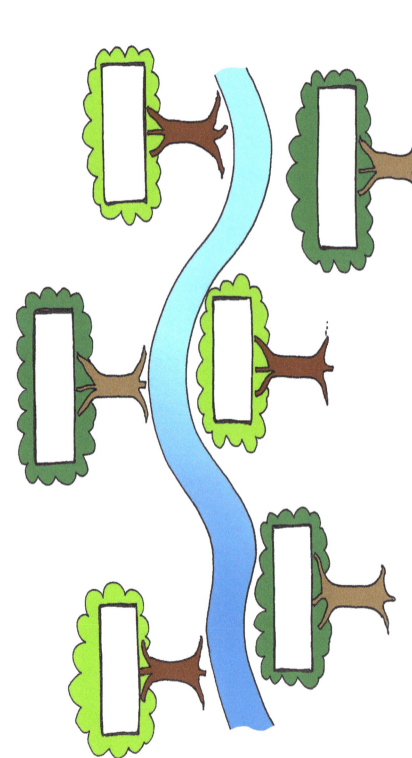

To achieve my dreams I could...

© 2017, *Talkabout Sex and Relationships*, Alex Kelly and Emily Dennis, Routledge

Activity 79 Top tips for looking to the future

Preparation

Worksheets should be printed out in A4 for individual work or enlarged to A3 for a whole group activity.

Instructions

- The group should come up with a list of top tips for looking to the future, thinking about the skills practised in this topic.

- You may wish to discuss these as a group first or group members can complete the sheet individually then share ideas after.

- This sheet can go in their individual work folders.

Activity 79 Top tips for looking to the future

Name: .... Date: ....

Top Tips

○

○

○

○

○

○

Remember:

Activity 80 Certificates

Preparation

Print out a certificate for each group member, add in names and sign.

Laminate the certificates if possible.

Instructions

- Hand out a certificate to each group member, one at a time, with a round of applause.

- You may wish to say one thing each group member has done particularly well as part of the relationships course.

- You may then wish to play a few group games to celebrate.

Looking to the future

Activity 80 Certificates

Certificate of Achievement!

Is awarded to

....

Congratulations

You have completed Talkabout Relationships!

Signed ....

Date............

⟨ⓧ⟩ Forms

Contents	page

1. Session evaluation   286

2. Parent/carer letter (under 16)   287

3. Parent/carer letter (over 16)   288

Forms

 Session evaluation

Group ....

Group members present ....

Date .... Session number ....

	Plan	Evaluation
Starter activity		
Main activities		
Finishing activity		

Completed by .... Date ....

Forms   **Parent/carer letter (under 16)**

Address

Date

Dear. . . [Parent/Guardian]

As you may be aware, we spend a lot of time supporting students to develop their interaction, confidence and friendships skills.

This term, we will be beginning group work with a number of students exploring friendships and relationships, including those of a more intimate nature with a key focus of staying safe. Topics will include: what is a relationship? How does a relationship begin? Relationship skills and looking to the future.

We would like to invite you to an information evening to discuss the details of what we will be covering in the groups and also answer any questions you may have. [Optional]

If you would **not** like your child to be part of this group, please complete and return the slip below.

In the meantime, if you would like to discuss this further please do not hesitate to contact me.

Kind regards,

[Your name]

I do not want my child . . . . to complete the above relationships group work this term.

Signed . . . .   Date . . . .

 **Forms**

Address

Date

Dear. . . [Parent/Guardian]

As you may be aware, we spend a lot of time supporting people to develop their interaction, confidence and friendships skills.

We will be beginning group work exploring different types of relationships, including those of a more intimate nature with a key focus of staying safe. Topics will include: what is a relationship? How does a relationship begin? Relationship skills and looking to the future.

We would like to invite you to an information evening to discuss the details of what we will be covering in the groups and also answer any questions you may have. [Optional]

In the meantime, if you would like to discuss this further please do not hesitate to contact me.

Kind regards,

[Your name]

TALKABOUT References and further reading

References and further reading

Kelly, A. (2016) *TALKABOUT: A Social Communication Skills Package* (2nd edition). Milton Keynes, Speechmark.

Maslow, A. (1962) *Toward a Psychology of Being* (2nd edition). London, Van Nostrand Company Ltd.

McCarthy, M. (1999) *Sexuality and Women with Learning Disabilities*. London, Jessica Kingsley Publishers.

Murray, J., MacDonald, R., Brown, G. & Levenson, V. (1999) 'Staff Attitudes Towards the Sexuality of Individuals with Learning Disabilities: A Service-related Study of Organisational Policies', *British Institute of Learning Disabilities*, December, 141–145.

Rubin, K. (2002) *The Friendship Factor: Helping Our Children to Navigate Their Social World and Why It Matters for Their Success and Happiness*. Middlesex, Penguin Books.

Wolfensberger, W. (1972) *The Principle of Normalization in Human Services*. Ontario, The National Institute on Mental Retardation.

Yacoub, E. & Hall, I. (2009) 'The Sexual Lives of Men with Mild Learning Disability; A Qualitative Study,' *British Journal of Learning Disabilities*, 37, 5–11.

Index

Index	Page
abuse	74–6
Abuse disclosure guidelines	10–11
Assessment	3, 13–24
attraction	166–8
Certificates	287–8
compliments	51
Compromising couples	281–2
Confidentiality	26, 37
Conflicting couples	225–6
Conflict – what should I do?	227–9
consent	95–101
conversation starters	183–5
Coping strategies	255–9
Coping with problems	221–45
Cupid's clues	186–90
Developing relationships	199–218
Different types of love	145–7
Emotional endings	253–4
emotions	28–9
ending a relationship	248–72
Fact finders	49–50
Fancy FACS	191–2
feelings	28–9
First date phases	193–4
Forms	4, 289–94
Getting to know us	25–54
Group rules	37–9
Heartbroken Henry	260–1
hierarchical approach to developing sex and relationships	5–7
How am I feeling?	28–9
How do we stay safe every day?	68–71

Index	Page
I have a dream	279–80
In full bloom	275–6
internet safety	104–19
Introduction to relationships	124–63
Jealous Jamal	235–7
Jealousy – what should I do?	238
Just around the river bend	283–4
Keep it real	107–12
Larry looks for love	180–2
Let it grow	199
letter to carer	4, 291–2
letter to parent	4, 291–2
Linked together	44
Little white lies	239–42
Looking to the future	275–88
love	143–8
Love grows	169–73
Loving life	269–70
Lying – what should I do?	243
Mates or dates?	159–61
Measuring outcomes	11
Mystery mates	113–17
OK/not OK	77–81
OK/not OK pictures	82–6
OK/not OK . . . take two	87–9
One nice thing	51–2
Overlapping relationships	133–4
overview of the book	3–4
Peer pressure – what should I do?	234
People in my life	130–2
Perfect partners	174–9
private symbol	34–6
Problem partners	221–4
Puzzle pieces	47

Index	Page
Qualities of a friend	135–9
Qualities of a partner	140–2
Relationship rules	162–3
Roll with it	152–8
Romantic rhymes	149–51
R U internet savvy?	118–19
rules for group	37–9
running a group	8–9
safe/OK/dangerous	61–2
Safety snap	63–7
See-saw of love	262–8
Session evaluation	290
Setting up and running a group	8–9
starting a conversation	183–5
Starting a relationship	166–96
staying safe	58–121
staying safe in relationships	72–3
Supportive signs	207–13
Talk tech	104–6
theory behind the book	1–3
This is a private group	34–6
This is me	45–6
Top tips for coping with problems	244–5
Top tips for developing relationships	217–18
Top tips for looking to the future	285–6
Top tips for starting a relationship	195–6
Top tips for staying safe	120–1
Top tips for when a relationship ends	271–2
trust	120, 200, 201
Trust obstacles	200
trusty detective	201–6
Under pressure	230–3
Valuing a partner	214
What could I do?	90–4

Index	Page

What does love feel like?	147–8
What does staying safe mean?	58–60
What is abuse?	74–6
What is attraction?	166–8
What is consent?	95–101
What is love?	143–4
What is relationships group?	30–3
What is trust?	102–3
What's great about being us?	53–4
What should Larry say?	183–5
When a relationship ends	248–72
Which is which?	124–9
Who am I?	40–3
Who is TALKABOUT Sex and Relationships aimed at?	4–5
Who's who?	48
Why might a relationship end?	248–52
Wonderful wishes	276–8